WARRIOR MOM

LONE SURVIVOR

TAME THE LIONESS HEART

WARRIOR MOM

LONE SURVIVOR

TAME THE LIONESS HEART

"If sharing my experiences on how I was able to overcome my life trials, I can save one single soul, it's more than enough accomplishment for me."

Authored by

Daisy Lozano Ludaes

Disclaimer

This book has been published with all reasonable efforts taken to make the material error-free after the consent of the author. This book is sold subject to the condition that it shall not, by way of trade or otherwise, be lent, resold, or otherwise circulated without the copyright owner's prior written consent in any form of binding or cover other than that in which it is published and without a similar condition including this condition being imposed on the subsequent purchaser and without limiting the rights under copyright reserved above, no part of this publication maybe reproduced, stored in or introduced into a retrieval system or transmitted in any form or by any other means without the permission of the copyright owner.

Registered Office- 907-Sneh Nagar, Sapna Sangeeta Road,
Agrasen Square, Indore – 452001 (M.P.), India
Website: http://www.wingspublication.com
Email: mybook@wingspublication.com

First Published by WINGS PUBLICATION 2024
Copyright **Daisy Lozano Ludaes** 2024

Title: **WARRIOR MOM LONE SURVIVOR**
Price: AED 60 | $17
All Rights Reserved.
ISBN 978-93-6006-517-1

LIMITS OF LIABILITY/DISCLAIMER OF WARRANTY

The Author of this book is solely responsible and liable for its content including but not limited to the views, representations, descriptions, statements, information, opinions and references. The information presented in this book is solely compiled by the Author from sources believed to be accurate and the Publisher assumes no responsibility for any errors or omissions. The information is not intended to replace or substitute professional advice.

The Content of this book shall not constitute or be construed or deemed to reflect the opinion or expression of the Publisher. Publisher of this book does not endorse or approve any content of this book or guarantee the reliability, accuracy or completeness of the content published herein and do not make any representations or warranties of any kind, express or implied, including but not limited to the implied warranties of merchantability, fitness for a particular purpose. The Publisher shall not be held liable whatsoever for any errors, omissions, whether such errors or omissions result from negligence, accident, or any other cause or claims for loss or damages of any kind, including without limitation, indirect or consequential loss or damage arising out of use, inability to use, or about the reliability, accuracy or sufficiency of the information contained in this book. All disputes are subject to Indore (M.P.) jurisdiction only.

James 1:2-6

"My brothers, consider yourselves fortunate when all kinds of trials come your way, for you know that when your faith succeeds in facing such trials, the result is the ability to endure. Make sure that your endurance carries you all the way without failing, so that you may be perfect and complete lacking nothing. But if any of you lacks wisdom, he should pray to God, who will give it to him, because God gives generously and graciously to all. But when you pray, you must believe and not doubt at all. Whoever doubt is like a wave in the sea that is driven and blown about by the wind."

Dedication

It's only but proper to dedicate this book to the most important and deserving people in my life. To my parents, Robles and Vilma, who taught me how to live and value life. My siblings and their spouses, Veran and Erlyn, Rex & Vi, Marie and Rich, Mel and Kat, Joy and Drew Jr., who all are so patient with me. They stood by my side and supported me without blaming or condemning me when I make mistake. To my nephews and nieces, Nyler, Renyl & Robyn, Alyn, Nica, RC, Zai, Pao & Xander, Nathan, AJ & Kovi, my inspirations. I'm keeping them always in my prayers to do better in their lives. And most of all to my son John Marc, my life, the reason why I stay alive. My strength every time I'm feeling down deep in the dark. And in memory of his younger brother, our angel, John Michael +. I can't stop thanking the Lord for giving you all to me.

Introduction

This book was a product of my life experiences put into reality out of my long time, dream of writing. Although it was put off for some time, it did not stop. I had been writing some of my life experiences and kept them aside but it never came into mind that it can really be published.

My work is physical and needs much of my time, so I never thought I could still find time to write and chase my dream. But it's not leaving me; it's just waiting for the right time. Until I got the needed help and inspiration. My coach and mentor found me at the right time. He helped me realized my dream and made sure that my work would be shared.

My life story, though, was too personal, but I believe that sharing it can be a way of helping others who are going through the same. I almost hit the end but I managed to come out from it. I came back and all I want to let you all know is that God grace is sufficient.

It is about my struggles regarding relationships, my battle with cancer, my spiritual life, financial issues, failures and how I was able to rise up and continue to live my life despite all those trials. And I know I can face them even if they keep coming to distract me.

It is a way of life. I learned to accept and live with it. I never lose hope because I know I'm not alone. Remember, if you give up, it's your loss. No matter what happens, kneel down, look up and pray. God is waiting for you.

Foreword

When I was transferred to another workstation, I left the place where I spent all my memories with my friends and co-workers. The place where I got all my scientific and practical experiences. It was hard at first to be relocated. Joining my new workplace, I realized that I have to live with the new environment and work with a new team, so I decided to immediately adjust and choose an administrative team that suits my ideas and aspirations in the art of management.

I started coexisting and getting to know the employees, and during my initial day-to-day encounters, it was Daisy, a very active employee, who caught my attention. I was impressed by her working habits, high ideas and goals, and she always seeks to develop and improve the quality of her work. I asked around, and her name was always mentioned and appreciated, so I asked her to join my new team.

In the beginning, we met so many challenges, but thanks to Daisy's wisdom, awareness and love of development, we were able to pass this stage easily. As days went by, I admired the way she answered emails and sent communications and the way she handled herself professionally when she talked during programs or meetings.

I compared Daisy to a rare, precious piece of gem. She

has a lot of talents and abilities that enable her to deal with employees easily, as well as her passion for writing and postal correspondence in a classy way.

One day I told her that she should be writing a book which she said it was her longtime dream. I gave her the idea at least to write her daily diary as she has a lot of beautiful memories and a sophisticated sense of presentation of topics, so this can qualify her as a writer. I told her to just go on enjoy writing and develop herself better. I support her in this realization of her dream to be a writer.

Mrs. Khawla Ali Taqi
HOU – LH CRA, Main Lab
DHA, UAE

Acknowledgement

It's always worth it that more than acknowledgement belongs to the one who is, above all, the Almighty God, the giver of my life and the source of everything, for without HIM, this book would never have happened.

And special mention to my coach and mentor, Dr. K., who unleashed the reins of my hidden treasure and awakened my strength and determination. He has the drive to help others and willingly shared and provided the exact structural guide we needed as beginners. He went out on his way to throw his net to catch people like me who have the passion to write but are just waiting to be found. No wonder he is so successful. And to his team, who provided full support until I finished writing this book.

Grateful also to all those who journeyed with me throughout my life. My relatives and friends who trusted me and have helped me in many ways, especially during my lowest moments. Not to forget my Bootcamp group, who persevered all the way to the finish line.

Special mention to my book writing Zoom mate Eva, we became very good friends in a very short time, we both empowered and supported each other day and night, learned a lot from each other and despite those distractions and destructions we met and experienced along the way, it will not stop us to chase our dreams because it's where we got the strength to persevere and inspiration to push us. We both agreed to continue to write books together.

Last but not least, big thanks to my immediate Emirate boss, the Head of Support Services Unit, Mrs. Khawla Ali Taqi, for appreciating my work and supporting my book.

Preface

I have always been dreaming of writing my own book. But I don't know what to write and how to write. I don't know when it exactly started. During my childhood, I developed this interest in reading, like local Comic magazines, then later Pocketbooks, Love stories, Mystery books and Detective stories. That dream was put off as I went on my higher studies. But for every stage of my growing up, especially if there's a particular event in my life that I've been through, I will go back to my dream of writing. It went on and off and remained as a dream.

I finished my studies and on to different levels and stages of my life, which I wrote about in this book. I may have not written any book, but I had this habit ever since that when I'm writing letters, notes, text messages, comments or emails, I always make sure of a good presentation, including grammar or spelling and only until I'm convinced of the correctness of it then I will proceed. This generation made it easy with the auto correction while typing.

Last January of this year, 2024, weeks after I just closed my business where I lost a large amount of money and was heartbroken that my aspirations had just collapsed in front of me, I decided to take a break, take a leave and sort of hibernate, de-stress, and divert my attention away from depression. Only God knows what I really needed at that time. No plans, all I know. I just needed a break.

Later did I know, I signed myself into a two-day Bootcamp I saw on Facebook about Book writing. Immediately, I told myself, this is it, I have so many things to write now, but no longer just for the sake of writing but through my experiences I know I can inspire others who are going through trials. Not to give up but to let them know that there is always hope, and I believe that they can overcome it too.

Content

CHAPTER 1

My Life of twists and turns

I can still clearly remember, it was early morning and still dark outside; I bid goodbye to my sweet, gentle, loving little boy, John Marc, half asleep on the sofa. Earlier that day, he said it was easy to wake up from the sofa to see me off. Yes, he agreed to my leaving, but I was not really aware of how long I would be away from him, though I already gave him a head start that I needed to leave and be away for work, the simplest way to explain, for the mind of his age, to understand. During that time, it was only him and me together but surrounded by overflowing family love and support. I left him under the care of my parents and a relative who took care of his needs at home and in school. It was the hardest part for me to know that my son went through a lot without me. And I don't have any other way to stop it. I was broken.

I had to travel six hours by land to reach the Airport, the same place where the agency I applied was located. The last time I was home, it took us barely three hours to ride from my home due to the government's improved infrastructure programs, I supposed. You can just imagine the times I spent travelling on the road back and forth during that time. A week before that, I received the news from the agency office that I have to leave the country within a few days. A couple of days back, I was in the same place completing all the requirements, then went back home, but I was asked a day before the flight to go back to their office again to do some tests and sign more documents, so I rushed back again.

I did not have the courage to talk to my son about the plan. Because there was no plan. It was sudden, and I didn't have time, so I had to leave immediately. Thus, it was his idea to sleep on the sofa to make sure he would see me when I left. I was coming back home in the middle of the night just to pick up my things and leave. That memory never left me until now and even how many times he came over to visit me here and came back for good to work. He stayed with me for quite some time until he got the job he had been dreaming of. He left for the US in 2021 during the pandemic. I wish I could turn back the hands of time. My only consolation was that he became the kind of person, my son I'm always praying for. He was not with me, and I'm not there during those times when he needed me but instead of worrying, all I did was to offer Him to God in my prayers to keep him safe always. He became a responsible man. He finished his studies without delay.

I reached the airport late due to the distance. Forever grateful to my cousins (we used their vehicle) and my dad, who travelled with me while my brother Rommel met us at the airport to see me off. Oh! I should not forget. We had an officer escort, my friend Cristina, but she had career shift, she's now also one of us exploring the world as a crew on one of the luxury cruises. Finally, all aboard, exhausted and seated comfortably on the plane, my mind wandered; I didn't know what was there waiting for me, but I was bound to the country I knew nothing about. I heard the paging system in a different language, which means we reached Riyadh Airport, Kingdom of Saudi Arabia. Then, via Domestic flight to Hail airport.

It was another full of unexpected ups and downs being new to the place, but overall, so many good things happened, too. I passed their licensure exam and worked as a Medical Technologist (Laboratory Technician). I completed only my two years contract. Looking back, I'm grateful to my cousin, Divina, who encouraged me to leave my comfort zone. She first got a job as a nurse and left before me to join her husband at his workplace. I followed later on but to another location far from them. As soon as I stepped past the Immigration officer, I was Officially added to the statistics of Overseas Filipino Workers leaving our country daily, bringing with us our different aspirations and purposes in life.

I learned so many of my firsts. Like sharing a room with strangers, later became my friends. Lived and worked with different types of personalities as well as Nationalities. My first time to learn a different language, Arabic, other than English as my second. Days went on, and it was not easy being away from home. Letters were still the means of communication at that time, and mobile phones for calling were quite expensive. Mobile cameras are still not allowed, and social media has not been used yet. I went home for a vacation after one year and the next year. There were so many reasons to consider, so it was hard for me to decide if I would go back to work. I asked for a six-month vacation with a promise to return, and they agreed. Though it was short-lived, I got loads of experiences that I can write about.

Only a few in my circle knew about this; going to Saudi was

not my first time to work overseas. During my younger years, I was introduced by a family friend to his aunt, the owner of a recruitment agency. Fresh from college and very young then, out of curiosity, instead of applying for a job related to my education, I followed my friends and relatives whom I helped to find a job overseas, I left for Hongkong and worked as a domestic helper. Yes, doing house help, I'm not ashamed; it's a decent job and for Filipinos, mostly the educated ones leave the country to work. Known now as caregivers, the most sought-after job that is paid well until now. You can meet nurses, teachers, and almost all the different bachelor's degrees working the same other than what they were schooled for. It is a sad reality that we have to leave our country either by choice or because not everyone can find a suitable job equivalent to their education back home. Work is a source of income, a means of survival. Unlike others, It's not always for luxury but for prosperity. Whether you like it or not, it fulfils a very basic need that has to be addressed. To have a roof over our heads, food on the table and clothing to cover ourselves.

That was three decades ago. My employer treated me well. But it didn't take long for me to work for them; no offence meant it, but my young mind just realized it was not the place for me. My employer even tried to convince me that soon their eldest daughter would study in London, where I could be with her or with the whole family if I stayed longer. They all are British citizens. Maybe it's a missed opportunity, but I believe it's apt to say it's not for me. That was the shortest time I spent as an employee, but I have a lot of memories of my weekend days off when I met friends and relatives and went to church. I gave them early notice to give them time. Soon, they got a replacement, so I did not complete six months and flew back home. Very short time, but I had gathered enough lessons, so I thought, I would cherish them for a lifetime.

It's worthy to mention that a few years later, I went back and revisited the place along with my son, John Marc and my two ever-loving, supportive sisters, Marisa and Ruby Joy, who were both single at that time. I attempted to find my employer, but for sure, they may have left already and be somewhere in another country. Being with my sisters and my son that time was an additional precious memory worthy to keep, which probably won't be repeated, as we live miles away from each other and time, family, and work will come in between.

Back home in the Philippines after I left Hongkong, I know I have to search for work to earn for myself and my son, not again to depend on my parents, after all they've already done their part. I got a job, contractual, in one of the government-owned agencies. Almost at the same time, I got married and blessed with a son the following year. It was a sudden turn of events, but I gladly embraced it, and from there, my life revolved only as a mother and as a wife. Work came next. It was not expected there was no more me and myself. I was just starting all over again, and I was caught unprepared for the next stage of my life, but life is like that.

I came to believe that there is no accident, regardless of age (legal age, it depends upon the culture and tradition), education or position, state of life, race or faith. But when it happens, there is no need to rush; planning is very important and necessary. Grateful to the Almighty God, of my family, they are always there to support me not only when I'm doing good but most especially each time I fail. When my son started school, I decided to leave my job and be a full-time mom to prepare his things and his food and to drop and pick him up to and from school. My husband was working then, but I did my best to find ways to help.

Six years later, I delivered my second son, a preterm baby, but lost him after two days. The unbearable pain of losing my other precious little one created a hole in my heart that almost tore me into pieces but was unconsciously masked by my strong personality. I have to be there for my other son, JM, barely six years old at that time, shattered upon learning that we lost his baby brother he had been wanting to have, hold, hug and to cuddle. It took him time to accept it too.

Marriage, is surely not only romance and happiness, it comes with great responsibilities that both parties will take care of. God did not promise us a life free of sorrows and tribulations. It's your call to stay and preserve the relationship. True enough, my relationship with my husband slowly turned upside down due to unresolved issues we both were not ready to face. We tried our best to save it but might not have done it the right way, we did not see the possibility of seeking help or we both did not take it seriously. I regret seeing my son suffer as a result.

We were not able to calm the storm we only created. Whatever may be the reason is immaterial anymore because before our tenth year of marriage we went our separate ways, it's me and my son together. Devastated and unprepared for what I called a new phase of life in shame from my surroundings, my family, relatives and friends, I saw myself lost along the way, spending more time with friends than with my son and family.

Through a friend, I found and started another job related to my previous job. It was then hard for me to start all over again with peace of mind. Not long after, I started working, that plan of going overseas again came to life. I thought I was not selected because my cousin already left some time ago and I never heard from the agency again. It was then a perfect time to go away far from the eyes of those who are feasting on my story, and that's when I found myself jumping again into the unknown, confused and unprepared, Saudi Arabia became my place of solace.

My Learnings

1. Don't Run from Your Problem. Face it. When you are in pain, broken inside, and you are trying to be strong, you don't immediately talk about your pain to your loved ones out of fear or shame. You just want to run away from the situation, so you jump on the first opportunity that takes you away from your problem and, worse, from your people. The only best way is to ask for help and talk to your family or any trusted person, for that matter. Asking for help during tough times, maintaining a good circle of friends who support you without judging you and having strong faith in God allows the pain to come out and can divert the course of things and lead you on a path where issues can be resolved and problems can be answered the better way, if not the best.

2. Listen to Yourself First, take time to decide. The pain is real. Initially, your mind is clouded, you feel numb, you can't think, you can't even eat or sleep, and you just wish that feeling would just go away. Some others go down at their lowest, they tend to oversleep and not want to get up, eat their problems away by binge eating. Worst, they end up on vices like drugs and alcohol. But deep down, your inner self is telling you, get up! You were a good person before this even happened. You were once hoping for a good life and on to a better future. You need to sober up and give yourself a chance to decide to better yourself. Wake up to a new day and greet the morning sun. It's easy to say, but there's no one who can help you at that very moment, only yourself. Keep going.

3. Plan the entire Path (Journey & Destination). A popular saying says, "If life throws you a lemon, make a lemonade". Never solve a problem with another problem, and always give some time to solve it. It's good not to involve others in personal issues, but talking to someone with a listening ear makes a difference. Prayer, of course, regardless of your faith, is very necessary and will do wonders, but you need to believe and nurture it to be able to use it effectively. God listens. You have to stop and think, look at the possible scenarios, the possible outcome of the decisions you will make, examine your conscience carefully, there should be no trace of doubt, that God is maybe talking to you, leading you to the direction to follow.

4. Ups and Downs are Part of Life. Because we are human, we are bound to keep working in order to survive. Thus, in the process, we take risks and commit mistakes because we always need to decide on things or matters in order to accomplish something. We will find out that not everything goes in our favour because we may be lacking in some ways or because we rush on things or we overdid them. If we base our decisions on our emotions, we will not be able to see the best in anything. There is the feeling of, "I'm not worthy", "I don't feel good with it", "I don't feel that is best", and so on. You can't decide because your reasoning is clouded by emotions. It's normal to find yourself once in a while feeling down, rejected, useless, broken, in darkness or almost worse, have given up. Never allow it. There's always hope; stand up and accept you make a mistake and work out it. If you leave it that way, you are making a big mistake. It's your call.

5. Meeting Different People and Learning Different Cultures. I get to learn about different kinds of characters, attitudes, cultures, and beliefs. It turned out that we are all the same in terms of how we live our lives and how we react to any actions or issues from each other in terms of relationships, friendships, work or just our everyday encounters. Leave the level of knowledge, wisdom or experience we will differ for sure. But I always believe in "good begets good" and "treat me well and I will do the same", but still, it can be on different levels because of individual differences. Each one is unique, no two people are the same, even twin siblings. "it's always better to be kind than to be right".

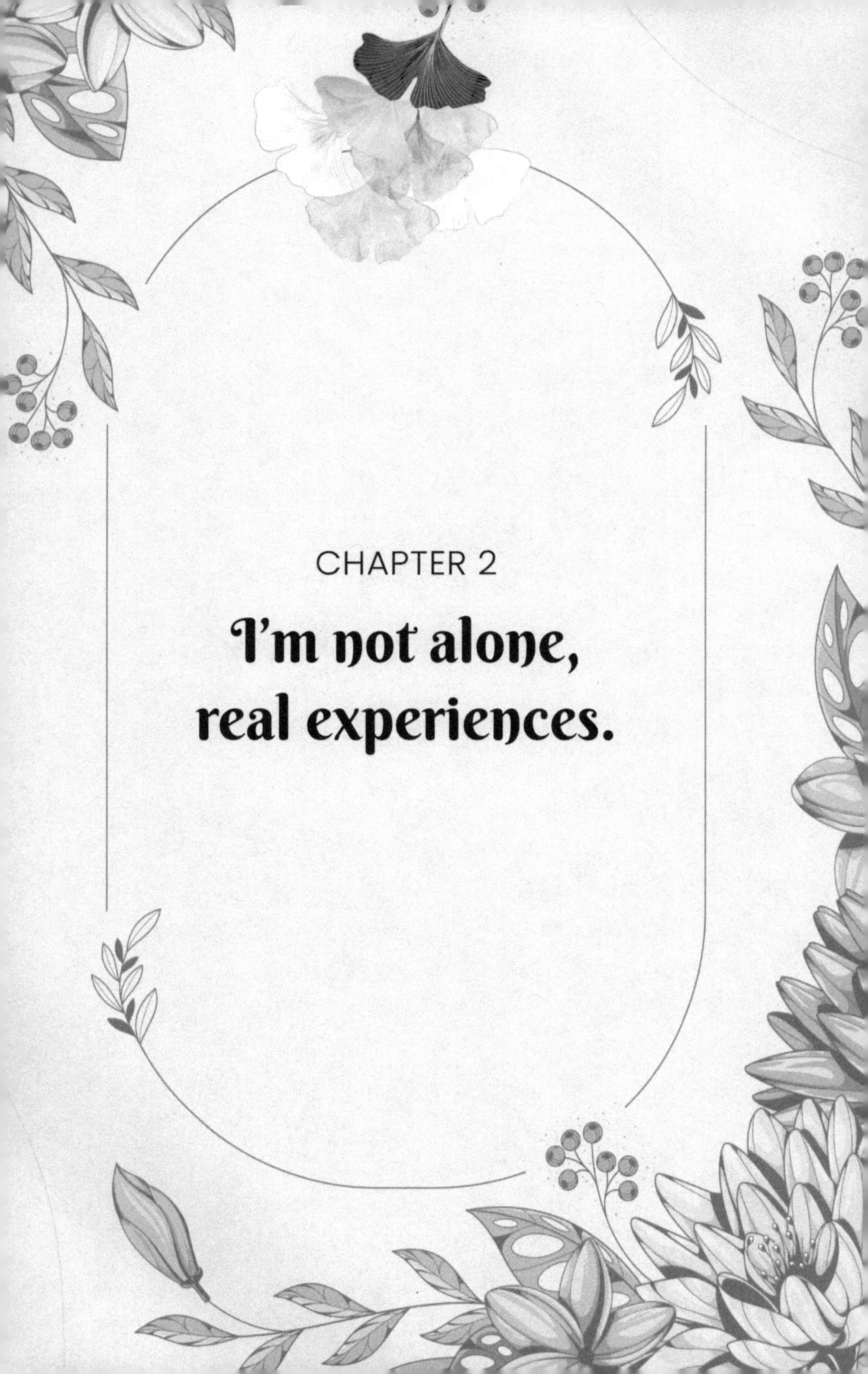

I'm not alone, real experiences.

Coping up is never easy; it takes time, and I have to admit help and support are necessary. Other than my own, I gathered strength from my family and friends; again, I saw the need to be strong for my son, who, again at an early age, received another and for sure, the biggest and hardest blow in his life when his father and I parted ways. I have no other way yet to explain to him further how and why it happened, and from that time, I know it left a void in his being that until now, as of this writing, I'm trying my best to fill it up again.

My family has always been my backbone, especially during those trying times; they stood by my side and made sure I would get back on my feet again. It was a long, winding road. It took me a long time nursing the pain, blaming myself and seeing myself as a disgrace to the family. I shun away from most of my friends, neighbors and even relatives. I kept a handful of friends near me whom I could run to when I needed someone to talk to, surprisingly, who also needed the same. Unknowingly, despite the failed relationship, while I was nursing and rebuilding my brokenness, I was also sharing myself, honest to goodness as to who I am, my strength as to what I can do and how I'm becoming as a person, as authentic as I can, I also became an inspiration and the strength to others.

Earlier on, I thought I was just pretending to be okay, feeling strong, but I'm really not or may have been faking it that I moved on, but I'm actually still trapped in the pains of the experiences I had. Then I proved myself wrong because I came to understand that something was going on beyond human power; there is higher up out there that was putting things in order no matter how messy things have become. Guiding my thoughts, guarding my steps that every time I lost my way, followed a different direction or reached a dead end, I'm always spared from more danger. Yes! That's where my strength is coming from. But it only became clear and was revealed to me as time went by. I learned that giving up is not an option. It's a grace you can't do alone. You have to be patient and learn. Rushing things will just make things worse. Take it slowly and surely because God is working on it. One thing is for sure, help is on the way. It might not be what or how we want it to be, but God always knows what is better, if not the best, for all.

For every mistake, I blamed myself. I thought, God knows when I did wrong or failed to make the right decisions, that's why I'm not blessed and that blessings were poured only to those who deserved them. I was wrong, because I knew by heart that God is love, merciful, and compassionate. He is not a punishing God! He gives second chances, lots and lots of second chances. But I should not take advantage of it. I should do better. Personal character, principles and convictions have an effect on the way we perceive and handle our own issues or how we fight our individual battles. The people we are with, including our family, and the situation we are in will also largely contribute. Even the environment, the place we live in, and the surroundings should not be ignored. But despite all the factors I mentioned, in the end, the person concerned has the decision to make. But it doesn't mean that I will no longer listen to other's advice or seek help. Will I face my problems or run?

My escape to reality, the second phase of my journey, started in KSA and continued until I came to the UAE. But mind you, life trials will never stop. It will come one after the other or will come at the same time. It might engulf you whole or in part, or it will help you surpass one after the other until you succeed. It may be to teach you a lesson and survive, or it can defeat you until you give up and end up a loser. It's your choice.

Yes! The struggle is so real. Mentally, emotionally, psychologically, physically and financially, I was tried and tested. Day in and day out, while I still have to deal with my excess baggage, even though it is hard, I still have to remain focused on my goal; no matter what happens, I have to send money for my son. I have to work hard.

One important thing is don't decide when you are not in your proper senses or when you're angry, disturbed or stressed. The probability of going wrong or following the wrong direction is very high. Be vigilant and cautious with the people you deal with or mingle with because each one is facing his or her own battle, and most likely, desperation can lead to something you will regret in the end. Life is beautiful, after all, no matter how hard it is. You may not see or understand how it works, but if you believe that there is someone up there who is bigger and has power above all, just do your part, believe and be patient, good things will happen.

When you are dealing with or talking to anyone at work or anywhere remember to treat them all the same like a family. Because one day, they can be the only ones who will be ready to help when you need it the most. It's not good to judge based on stereotypes or character, especially unpleasant, that is attached to any race or culture for that matter because we all are capable of change or improvement. I got to meet so many awesome, wonderful, kind, respectable and loving people, so many of them, and to some, I became a member of their family. We learn from our mistakes, from the not-so-good things we saw, and from our experiences, and we can use them to our advantage and be a better person today than yesterday. Regardless of the differences, we can still make the world a better place.

We dream, we overcome struggles and we make it. Work hard, learn from successful people, learn from mistakes, and have the heart to share your blessings, not only materially; it can be your talent or wisdom or your time. It's not the amount of money, state of life, position or material things that measure success. You can be living a simple life and you can feel successful. Contentment and feeling joyful despite the difficulty you face every day is what really counts. You may have everything, but you are drowning in debt. You may be the best in what you do, but you create more enemies. You may be a very good leader, but your family is shattered. And so on and so forth. The journey of a thousand miles begins with but a single step". Start small to prepare you for the big ones.

I don't pretend, I've mastered the art of masking up my emotions. After giving myself time to grieve over any misfortune, I know I need to live not only for myself but for my son, most especially; he is my only treasure, a precious gift from God that I can only call my own and whom I can fight for until the end. Then for my family, who stands by me through thick and thin; though I failed them many times, they will never turn their back on me. I love them so much. I missed every moment I get to spend with them, which is always short but memorable since me, my son and some of my siblings and my parents relocated abroad to different countries. And yes, I have to live for my friends, too, who also love me to the core and who can't lose me. I feel I have a responsibility to fulfil the friendships that I built. It could be anywhere, be it in school, at work, in church or just outside my home. My family knows how important friends are to me; they have known me all throughout to be always surrounded by friends of different kinds, and they know I'm well taken care of because I always value friendship that has no end. It just came to mind. I never had a best friend, as in the real meaning of one best friend whom I can run to anywhere and anytime I needed help or vice versa, but I do have friends who, at one time or another in my life, acted as one in the real sense even though we don't often see each other or communicate to each other. True, I never get to have that one and only best friend, but I'm blessed with so many friends who are ready and willing to give their best. Just by being me and who I really am, with confidence and kindness and a ready smile for them, even if my heart is dying inside.

I was separated early on, which is one reason why I left the Philippines, but the annulment of the marriage came a little later. I discovered that I was not alone, so many relationships were falling apart and there were so many broken families, not to mention broken children out of that. I was not aware of this, although I've been hearing some stories, for the main reason that I never exposed myself outside since I got married and especially when I had my son to take care of. I only go to work and be home to be a plain housewife and a mother. I don't have time to meddle with others' affairs. I kept mine private as well. I totally withdrew from the usual active and extrovert life I had, sort of carefree but fully guarded by my parents' words of wisdom and guidance. But it was not a guarantee all would be good. I still failed in many aspects of my life.

I made a mistake. Yes, but it doesn't mean I'm a bad person. It should not affect my whole being and how I relate or deal with other people I met or anyone for that matter. That's how I win friends, my genuine and authentic character, it's a grace from above. They say crying is a form of therapy because it releases stress and tension. In my early encounters, I cried a bit, sometimes I cried maybe more, but as far as I can remember, I never cried for all what had happened to me, strange? Maybe because of the saying, "Don't cry over spilled milk". Or maybe I just learned also the art of coping up under stress. Crying alone will not solve issues. Pray for guidance and stay strong. Admit you make mistakes and correct them. Learn to forgive others too.

I've been super active in my younger years. Even though mom was not really into my sports, she appreciated my accomplishments but never stopped telling me her concern over my safety after every competition, "What if something happens? Who will take care of me?". I played Judo, the art of gentle way, at YMCA of Baguio City. I was actively competing during my college days representing the University of Baguio, Baguio City and the Province of Benguet. After college, priorities changed until it can no longer fit into my mom and son's activities so I gave it up. My friends are still actively involved and plays up to this date or as playing coaches. They are still making names together with the next generation along with their children. I'm happy for their success, too. While my son in his younger years joined the Karate club. In one of his short visits here in the UAE. I enrolled him in a karate club in Sharjah and he was lucky to join in one Karate Tournament. He won a medal in the Kata competition. No doubt I'm the mother of my son. This reminds me, one time he asked me, "Mommy, do I look like you, or do you look like me?". I smiled he didn't know how happy I am to be acknowledged.

After college, I was not able to find time to meet and catch up with any of my classmates and friends. Everyone was busy chasing a dream or starting a family, and so was I. Until we all lost contact and could no longer see each other. While those who were nearby became unreachable, too. Mobile phones were not yet invented at that time. But now especially with the power of social media friends or people once forgotten or who were just hard to find are popping out one after the other. Friends I met later on became all an important part of my life as like those friends whom even I'm not seeing or seldom I see or lost contact with are still considered as treasures that when found their value remained. And like family, they are always there too. One good thing about social media is that it brings back people we haven't seen for a long time, reminds us of forgotten past, and rekindles precious memories.

It's never too late to begin. Capitalize on what you already have, your learnings, talent or passion. Ask for help and guidance from the right people. I've been there; I kept postponing my ideas, thinking I was not yet ready and lost another opportunity. Because I didn't have the means, my mindset was I could only do a few things, so in the process, I kept losing whatever little I made. What about if I dream big? Yes, I can, and you can do it too. Go slow, don't rush and do it with proper guidance, but you have to start now. Don't get stuck in the dreaming part of the planning process. Just do it. Don't delay.

I too, procrastinated for some time. It didn't help. When you are in the middle of something or whatever you are doing, and you feel it's not working when the data is not showing well, or after all you have done, you know something is not fair and, worse of all, you failed. You did not only fail; that failure of whatever you are doing, a relationship or a business, means you failed your loved ones too. Now you will feel it's only you against the world. It will slow you down, and you take it all against you, blame yourself, and you will start to believe you cannot do much. You will not even like to wake up anymore to a new day. You keep thinking, but your mind is empty. The consequence of the failure is eating you. And you feel you are at the edge. You are face to face with a wall, and there's no way out. It's at this moment that depression will set in. Don't even allow it; easy to say, I know, but you have to fight it. Don't ever dwell on it or keep it to yourself. Immediately ask or look for help, again from the right people. Don't ever give up! Never.

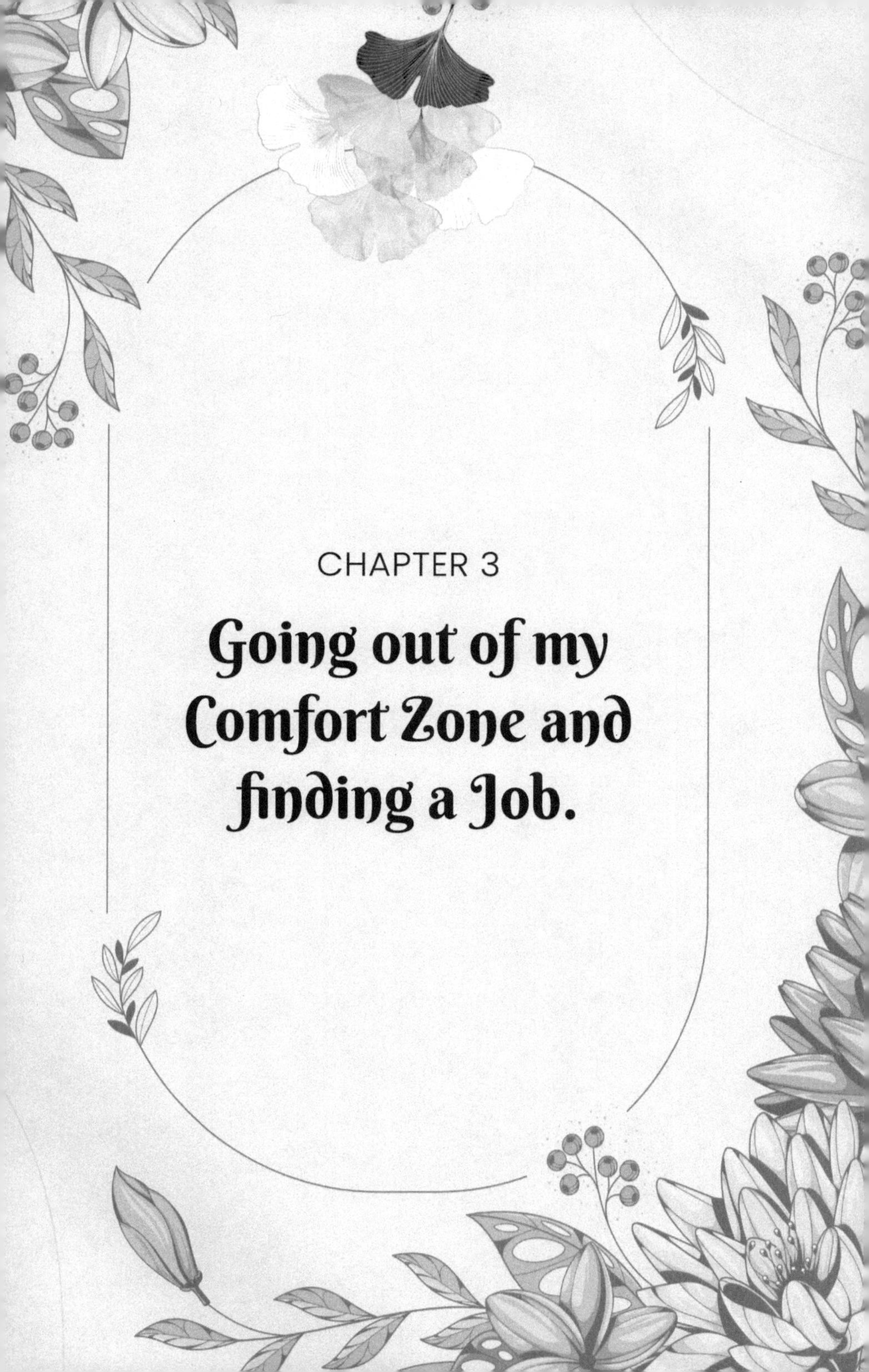

CHAPTER 3

Going out of my
Comfort Zone and
finding a Job.

Clearly, I did not go back to KSA. After a couple of months of trying to readjust back home, still confused and thinking about what to do next, I needed to find a job and start all over again. I woke up one day and realized I had to do something. Looking back, it was a wasted time. I did not accomplish anything. I was still in my darkest moments, convincing myself to live up to expectations, trying to show I had already moved on and came up stronger but actually still broken inside. The only good thing was being physically back with my son. Two months before my Saudi Iqama (working permit) expired, through the generosity of my sister Marisa, I packed my things and left my son again. Instead of going back to Saudi Arabia, I landed in the UAE.

I arrived on a summer time with a temperature reaching 50 degrees (it was a different experience then in KSA), I have no idea at all what I'm going into, my mind is still wandering. As soon as I got out of Dubai airport, I was led to an old villa-type house in a small room with 3 double deck beds prepared for 6 persons. No attached kitchen, it was just a makeshift outside the room. And the old AC was almost falling down, it hardly produces cool air. My space will only be my bed and a place for my bag. The space left in between the beds was for the small table we used for eating.

That was way back in 2006. I decided not to leave Dubai, though I can still go back to Saudi; my visa is still valid. I don't know where and how to start, but what was certain at that time, it was the start of a real struggle. I heard about Dubai for the first time when I was in Saudi Arabia after watching a movie from a recorded copy. I did not bother to gather information about what I should expect or at least do research to know more about the country. I never knew that I would be coming here.

With a limited amount of money at hand, all I prayed for was to start working immediately. I have to start earning and be able to send money for my son. I found out not all are lucky enough to reach their goals the way they wanted them to. Some were hired immediately after an interview in a day or two, in a week or month, but it took me six months at least for the job that suited me after working for some office part-time jobs. Sadly, I was not paid enough for my part-time jobs to cover my expenses because I'm not a permanent employee and on a visit visa. Although it was a temporary position, I worked for one full month. This happens when the staff is going on annual leave, they need a temporary replacement but they will not pay the full salary. Still grateful I was able to manage.

It was a roller coaster ride when I started searching for a job. I have no laptop so I need to go to the computer shop. I have to rewrite and edit my CV and send it to different companies that, most of the time, were not read at all or my job description does not suit them. I prepared according to my experiences and the work that I can do to have a higher chance of being hired. The hassles of going for interviews face to face or by phone. A few good Samaritans offered some help, like transportation and a few dirhams even if they need it too and helped us with getting through the situation like they did. Giving information and directions or referring us to employers or people they know who can help. God bless them wherever they are. I wish them success, too, in all their endeavours.

The second part time work I had was referred to by the first one. I had funny experience here. I waited for some time to receive my pay; I was so excited and happy; they added 50% to that first pay check, enough to cover my transportation. Obviously, I didn't have a bank account yet, so she changed the cheque to cash but borrowed the additional 50%. I had to return the next month to get it back. I needed the money, but I supposed she needed it more than me; she had just returned from leave. It is expected anyone who goes back home will bring everything on hand, not only for the family but also for the neighbours, and will surely come back empty. She knows very well that I'm still searching for a job on a visitor visa.

I lived in a room for six or more people. Others experienced living in the same size of a room with eight or ten people depending on the need or situation. They can add more bunk, folding or double-deck beds. To save money, two people can squeeze themselves and share the same single bed. Some have split duties, so one will use it in the morning while the other is at work and the other's turn during the night, and vice versa. This applies not only to those who are still looking for a job but even to those who are already working in order to save more money. A very tough life.

No turning back. Every day with my roommates, who had no job yet, and some neighbours and their friends went out together or sometimes on our own to hunt for jobs. Most of those in the sales will try a day or two. When they don't feel like it, they will not go back and join us again. In the process, when faced with uncertainties, we gradually lose patience, hope, courage and faith, especially when we are running out of hope. To each his own, help is nowhere to be found. My heart was tested many times, even when I knew I needed it too. When someone asks for help, I can't help but share what I have. I usually end up in debt. This character has gotten me many times in more trouble rather than in a good situation. But God took care of me. I get to meet so many people with so many different challenging stories. Even though I worked for some time in Saudi Arabia, Dubai is totally different. Where it is located, what it is like or the rules and practices. I should have known all these or at least something about the people and the food of the place I'm visiting and intending to live in before coming.

One of my friends asked me why I always go to church instead of looking for a job, just like asking why I am wasting time praying. My only answer was because I needed it. Although they do come with me to church during weekends. This is the best thing and I love most here in the UAE. They initiated, supported and strongly promoted the spirit of co-existence, tolerance and equality. Thus, we can freely practice our faith.

Worthy to note that when I first came here to the UAE, with me on the plane was Naira, we had almost the same agent so we were placed together in one flight but we separated in Hong Kong with a different flight to Dubai, we met again and ended up living in the same place. With her was Sally, who obviously became our first friend before even reaching UAE. She immediately took time and showed us around, including the church, and helped me reunite back to the same community I had back home, the Couples for Christ. I joined the Handmaids of the Lord. Sally, once in a while, during her day off, would accompany us or treat us somewhere, and we would bond together. After some time, Sally and her family left the UAE. Naira also got married to Ice, a friend we met here in Dubai, and then later, she decided to go home. Once she came back to join her husband and work again. I remember the last time we were together when I got sick, they both came and cooked for dinner that we shared. Later on, she decided to go home for good. They now have two kids and are enjoying a happy, content family life. Most of those I first lived with are now successful, building their families and living their own lives, each to their chosen paths in different parts of the world. But some of them did not find work and went back home. I believe God has something better for them, too.

One thing is for sure that from all these events collectively, we have learned so much from each other and, in one way or the other, may have led each and every one to our destiny. Wherever they are now, we all made a difference in each other's lives. People come and go in our lives. Someone will go today, and another one will come, but life will not begin or stop with them. As the saying goes, "They come either to teach us a lesson or to stay and be part of our lives". On the other hand, everyone's goal of leaving home to any place abroad is all for financial fulfilment, either for themselves or for their family. Most of the time, due to desperation, some will do everything to reach their goal. And as soon as they find a job, they try to work it out to their advantage.

So many have already proven that doing their best will most likely lead to success, but also, most of the time, it's not true for all. As they go along, it seems even with the jobs that they have, life becomes harder, and the needs are bigger than how much they can cover. The reason why some people resort to multiple jobs or part-time. And that's when the bank comes in, offering loans and credit cards that, when not well managed, put most people in trouble. Sometime before, it was almost for everyone, easy to have one. Now, it's based on the salary bracket, making sure of the capacity of the borrower to pay. But still, so many are hooked on taking salary loans and credit cards due to necessity but for others only to maintain their high standards of living even if they can't afford them. If they can manage well, it will be a good help, or else, instead of solving their problem, it will make it worse.

You want to know if I also use credit cards? Yes, I used to have cards. Not only one or two, but I also had three credit cards at the same time. I always had them, and over the years, I tried to manage them, hardly though, until it went down to only one, which I just got rid of recently by converting it to a regular loan. It was my only help during those times of financial crisis, but I made sure that only when very necessary. It was never for my personal wants, like having the latest gadgets to be on trend or buying expensive watches, bags, clothing, or shoes. I never had one of those that I bought on my own, and even if I have the means, I will never buy them. I guess because that's how I was brought up. My mom always tells us, "Buy what you need and not what you want". Thanks to my parents, who are my role models. It is also interesting to note one of my happiest moments that the only time I get to try a few of those luxuries, or the signatures, known brands, of course, they are to me, even not the most expensive things, is when my sister or my mom will give me or when I receive as a gift from my well to do aunts or sometimes from friends. I never spend on unnecessary things especially using a credit.

I should not give the idea that the reason why I sound broke even if I got a job is because of my credit card. Well, my pay is not even enough to maintain my own flat, but I know I need a decent home to stay and rest, at least because this is my home now. I'm not buying the idea that it's okay to live an uncomfortable life here because it's just temporary. We will later go back home to a good and comfortable life. That will not be the case. Anything can happen anytime that will change the course of life. I learned to live in the present because tomorrow is another day. I'm one of those who are doing their best to make a difference. I work my best but I don't expect much in return and I don't fight when others get promoted ahead of me. It's just not my time I believe. I don't like to compare I'd rather say I need it but they need it more than me.

When I first came here, I experienced having very little space for myself and living almost like inside a jail because you can't do what you wish to do. I made my way out to having my own flat. It took me so much time, sweat, courage and lots of sacrifices before I was able to make it. Yes, my salary still can't afford it and it is too big for me. I had to share my flat, but not for business purposes. I also made sure that it welcomes everyone like a real home away from home. I know I can't afford both a home and a car (I can if I take a loan), but if you ask me, I would rather choose a place to stay where I can sleep and relax than own a car and live in an uncomfortable home.

Even honey bees and birds made their way onto my porch to co-exist and built their families. I also had indoor plants, but the last time I put them out, the birds ate them all. I had to master tolerance, too. The latest addition to my family, I finally kept fish in my little aquarium. As of this writing, I'm thinking of putting a screen on the porch because the birds keep coming back, and it's hard to clean their litter. The second two birdies just learned how to fly a few days ago, I had to help them fly fast hoping they would leave so I could clean but again, I saw 2 eggs just waiting to be hatched. There will be a total of six birdies hatched in my home after this. I want to keep them in an open cage because I know they will keep coming back, but I don't know if it's legally allowed. My porch is their home. They felt safe. I have to wait for them again until they learn how to fly. And no more eggs, please! I used to watch them while I was writing.

While the honey bees, the first time they invaded my porch, I let them stay for some time, but I agreed with my nephew Bruce Jr. to put them away for fear of being bitten; I was actually bitten, but I did not tell them. It sneaked past through the screen door. Later on, a second batch came back. I decided to just let them stay, but they were on my glass sliding door, which I believe is not suitable for them, so they slowly left; most of them dropped and, like their Honeycomb, just dried up. They, too, have equal rights to live just like us, wander like humans in search of survival, and settle where it suits them as long as they feel safe with their surroundings. Thanks God. He takes care of the birds and the bees, or else I can't support them either. Well, again I was using my card only for emergencies and important bills to pay when my salary can't cover it all. For tickets or visas when I'm going on vacation or when my son is coming to visit me. And when I buy his stuff for school, clothing or when he runs out of allowance. No extra budget for extra mouth to feed.

You might disagree but going home for vacation without money on hand, to some, is shameful, at least for most of us living abroad. That's why we can't often go home as much as we want to. Those who do surely have not much left in their savings, too, unless they are really rich. But again, no money can equal the value of being with the family and spending precious time with them, even for a short time. It is a way of life we embrace in order to survive; it's the support that one can give in exchange for being away from the family that matters more. An expensive reality that is hard and painful to accept. That's why I always try to make my annual vacation possible to coincide with my family's vacation so we can bond and get together, but it does not always happen. And when I'm with my siblings and parents, they get to pay most of our expenses while I pay less because that's all I can afford. More than that means more use of my credit cards and more to pay when I go back to work. The worst scenario for us expatriates is a never-ending cycle; when one is trapped in debt, it's difficult to get out.

My story will tell you and will let you feel how it is to be in a different place so far away from home alone and how to live your life faced with challenges that may drag you to the edge, strip you of your dignity, and you still have to stand up and fight until the end what you believe is best for you. I learned my lesson the hard way. Your experience may not be the same as mine, but those lessons I gained may help you, too.

At the end of the day, you have to ask yourself. Why are you here on earth? There should always be a purpose. Have you at least reached your goal for the day? Always remind yourself of that purpose. It may be to be successful not only in having a job but through it, you can financially support your family, especially growing children or ageing parents. Or by having a good position where you can be able to help others too. The purpose or reason why you do your best and make sacrifices must always be your guiding wisdom to keep you focused and fixed on that goal and fulfill it. Without purpose in life living is useless.

Manage your finances. Identify your needs and avoid your unnecessary wants, especially if they are obtained by using credit card. It's ok to say no if you can't afford it. Save first and buy them later and not the other way around. Avoid promotions and discounted prices because the interest on the credit card is way higher than the discount you believe you will save. And if you wish to help others but you can't or don't have the means, you are not obliged to give. Don't force yourself. It's good to help, but let's learn from experience, borrowing from others, especially with interest in order to help others, and worst is when you use something you have that is intended for a different purpose because you want to help, will surely put you in big trouble. Your only way left is to pray for those in need that help will come at least from people capable of helping them.

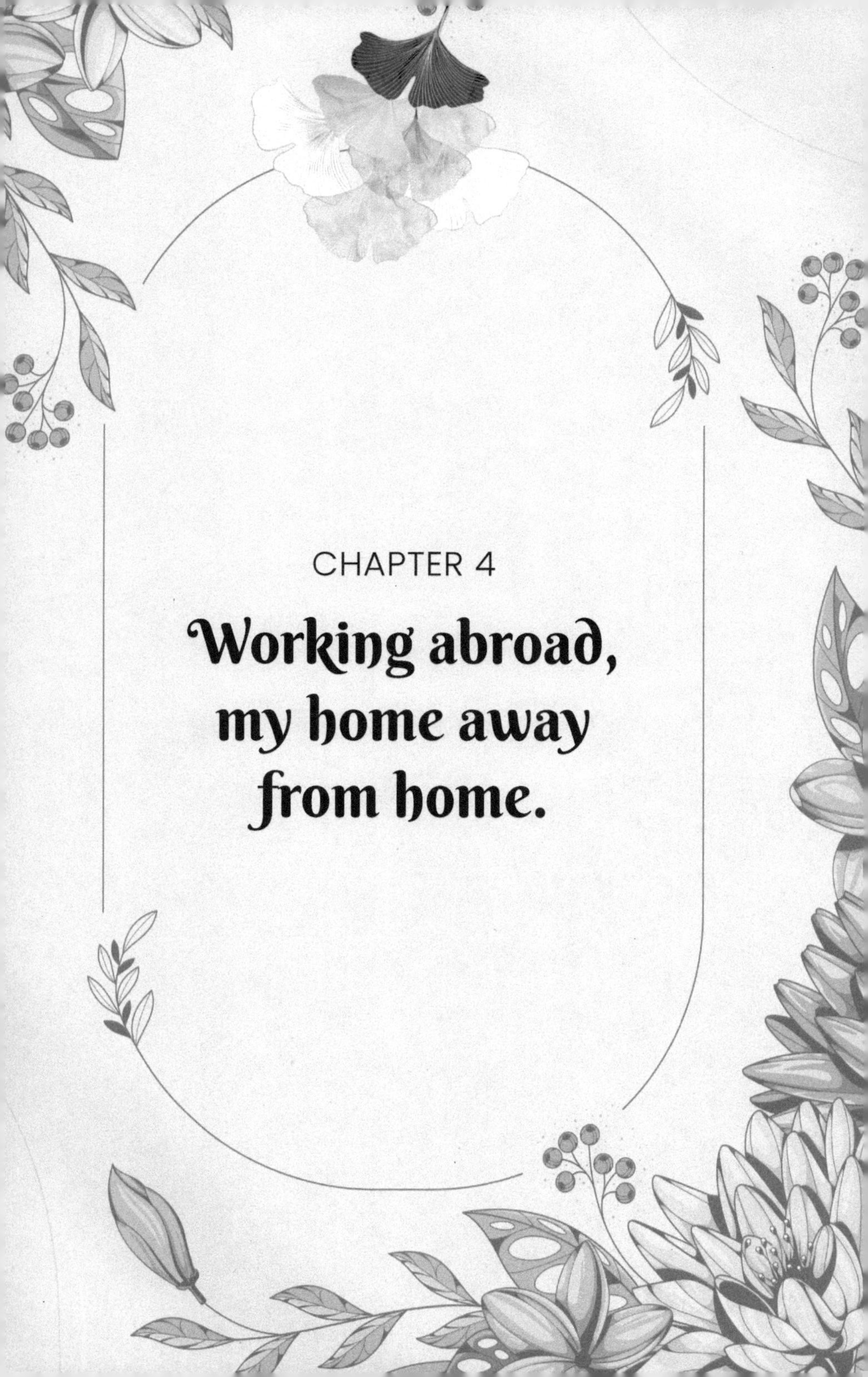

Working abroad, my home away from home.

The long wait was over. Five months later, it was November of 2006, I received the most awaited call for an interview in one of the hospitals here in Dubai. I was working then in one of the hotels as Secretary to the General Manager for a month. It was a no-choice situation; I thought I would not get the chance to apply my profession anymore. I was hired by the hotel when my visit visa was near to expire. I just renewed my visa under the hotel's name but at my expense. The day before that, I submitted my documents to HR so they could process my working visa. Can I get it back before they will even process it? I was so confused.

Before that call, I went on exit for my visa change. Unfortunately, someone took my mobile at the airport. One beautiful girl (different nationality) sat beside me and was talking to me for some time; she told me a story that seemed believable. Accordingly, her former local employer will marry her, so she needs to change visa and go back to be his wife. Absurd, actually, but I'm new. I don't know the rules, so I put off my critical thinking. Besides, I have my own issue to resolve. But I wondered why she did not leave at the time she told me her flight schedule? As soon as she left, my new mobile was also gone. It took me about a week to come back because it was Ramadan, less working hours, visa processing was expected to be delayed. Thankfully, I was with a group of good guys, so there was nothing to be afraid of, thinking of those scary stories we often hear from others, which I don't like to talk about here. Some others who need to change from a visit visa to a working visa will take 14 days, the allowable days to stay and sometimes more, so they are obliged to renew their visit visa in that country until they receive their working visa. I did not contact anyone, not even the hotel where I was working until I came back and told them the story. I immediately got a new phone and decided to retain my contact number, but it will be reactivated only after 24 hours. Without that same contact number, there's no way I would be contacted by the hospital.

I got no other choice left, I accepted my fate to work in the hotel with the agreed amount of salary, which was not enough, but with free accommodation, free food because I can eat with the guests and also free transportation. I will just figure out later how to survive. What is important then was to have a working visa and to stop spending on visit visa renewal, or else it means going back home. That was mostly the mindset of someone when faced with the same situation as mine. That call changed everything. The instruction as to when and how to go to the hospital were very clear. Early in the morning, I will go to the main lab and look for a certain person. I guess I can finish the interview early and I can go back on time for my work. No need to ask permission, or I will be in trouble. But I informed one trusted colleague. I just felt someone should know where I am. So I went, waited for some time, did the interview and left immediately. I was back to work on time. However, as soon as I opened my phone, which I kept silent during the interview, I saw four missed calls. I chose one to call back, and the secretary answered. "Where are you? We've been calling you. You have to come back to sign the papers, or you will lose the job!"

My heart was pumping, it was almost time for my work, but I couldn't afford to lose the chance of finally working in a hospital. I called the same colleague and told him about it, he gave his full support. There was no way to waste time, and he was almost pushing me to rush back to the hospital. I will never forget when he reached into his pocket and handed me 100 dirhams to take a cab and go back to sign the documents. For a while, I forgot about what would happen if I go back late and if my boss would know about this job interview after submitting my documents to them. My prayer was, "If this is Your will for me, then be with me". I went back and signed the documents. Because I want to save money, especially it's not mine and I should pay it back, so I decided to take the bus. It's just near, I thought, my bad, it was very heavy traffic on my way back and the bus was nearly not moving. Then I realized it was a Thursday, it was a regular meeting day in my work calendar with a very important agenda because not only the PRO but the Owner of the hotel would be joining, and maybe my manager was happy to introduce me as the new addition to the family, just I thought. I was taking it lightly, but deep inside, I was dead nervous until I reached and got back to my table, I couldn't pull back my mind to focus and work.

I can feel the tension between me and my boss, although I asked for an apology I didn't receive a nice response. He became busy the whole day in a closed-door meeting with the Owner, so I was just waiting and passing the time in between work so I could find a good time to talk to him at the same time, thinking about my interview and the next step I should take. They were not done until I asked to go home. He just told me to carry on, as his usual daily after-work send-off words and take note, with a big hug, which I feel is awkward, but I believe without malice. This time, there was none, I felt better, but that proved that he was upset about what happened. I went home, and I was starting to prepare myself for the worst encounter ever with my boss the next day. He was good to me and not to brag, but from the day I joined, he knew I could be an added asset to the company. He always tells me I'm holding a good position next to the General manager, and I just reply with a smile. And now I'm leaving them very soon for good. I wish I could still work until I start at the hospital, but I'm very sure then it will not happen.

When I signed the documents at the hospital, it was as good as I was hired, and that was the confirmation. Initially, I didn't have plans yet to inform my boss. I can wait until my working visa is processed; then, that's the time I will leave to secure my salary and support myself while waiting. But they have my passport and I need to submit it to the hospital HR as soon as possible to process my visa. I didn't sleep the whole night. I need to talk immediately to my boss or else I will regret it later on. I prayed, "If again I will make a mistake (leaving the hotel job) and make a wrong decision (I still can't fully believe I'm already hired), please give me courage and sustain me so that I will be able to find a job again". I'm already feeling I'm on a dead end, and thinking about it, I will again borrow money. Moreover, going back home is no longer an option. I kept it to myself. I did not inform my family until I got the job. The next day, I'm sort of prepared for the consequence, but I can feel butterflies in my stomach. On my way to work, rehearsing the words in my mind as to what I would probably tell my boss and how I would explain to him what had just come up. The only reason is that it was really the work I'd been longing to have; thus, the sudden change of my mind. That thought made me more anxious. But of course, I will not deny the reason that the pay will be better, not the best though. What if he will not allow me? or might create trouble like the stories I usually hear shared from others' experiences? The more I became agitated and rattled.

Seated at my office table exactly in front of the office of my boss, the Hotel General manager, I tried to act as normal as I could. I reached earlier before him. I did my usual early morning work and activities. My colleague handed me the menu of the day so I will prepare the food labels to be printed. I created my own design every day to make it look attractive for the hotel guests. Then, I book hotel guests arranged by the PRO, either as visit or transit visa. Check email communications especially those that needed immediate reply. Answer inquiries. I made myself busy to calm myself and pretended everything was okay until my boss came. As soon as he finished his daily update and instructions, he went inside his office and closed the door. By then, I had already made up my mind. I have to act now. I immediately drafted my resignation letter. I did not think about what would happen next. All I was thinking was to take back my passport and documents so I could bring them to the hospital. I waited for the right time; either I would wait for him to come out, or I would knock on his door. I carefully printed my resignation letter. It's full of heartwarming apologies and thanks. But as soon as I handed it to my boss and with a very faint voice, I said, "I'm sorry", he snapped. I just listened and took everything he said.

He did not read my resignation letter, instead called the PRO and told him what happened. He said he already knew it when I came late the day before. After they were done talking, the unexpected words from the PRO shocked me. It was almost noon, supposed to be our lunchtime but I did not feel hungry. "You must go exit today!" Go and bring your ticket, show it to me, and the driver will bring you to the airport, where you will only be handed your passport". I was totally stunned and almost fainted in front of them. First, clearly no flight at that time and second, where will I bring money for my return ticket and new visa? I just did it a few days ago. Coming back to my senses, weakened by what I've heard, the only reply I told in my rattled mind, I really don't know how but with a very low voice, trying to stay as calm as I could to control my emotions, I looked into his eyes and said, "Sir, can I go tomorrow?". The informal meeting adjourned. Within a few minutes, I was walking out the hotel, the world turned upside down again. I used to walk home but my mind was so busy, so I took the bus instead. I called for rescue from friends.

The words of my boss lingered from time to time in my mind. It took me a very long time to forget. I've always wished to go back one day and meet him to make peace and lessen the guilt I kept for a long time, but it did not happen. I went back one day, but he was not there; they purchased another hotel, so he was there that time. I met with this former colleague and paid him back. What happened that time came out of disappointment as he said it. I admit I was hurt by the words he blurted out because I didn't do it intentionally, no hidden agenda or plan that I could leave anytime; that's why I gave my documents so that they could process my visa with them. I tried to explain when I went back to collect my passport and document that I don't intend to cheat or trick them into hiring me just for my own advantage, that the offer came unexpectedly so I had to decide quickly. I was doing it not for myself but for my son. He understood and give me his big final hug.

That day, as soon as I left the hotel, I called my agent and told her the story. I need to exit again to change my visa. Although I paid that visa, it was under the hotel's name, so my boss said, "you can't go around looking for a job using our visa". My agent understood my situation, she told me to go ahead and she will book a ticket. I told her I still need to arrange for the payment. She agreed that I could leave even before giving the payment. My cousin Erich will hand it to her when completed from the friends I called. Though this is another tough struggle, one good thing was, it is worthy to remember, it will be my last and final exit to change my visit visa. My cousin Erich and my friends pulled together the cash to finance my plane ticket, which I paid back later on an instalment basis. I would be glad if at least one of them would read this. They all know how they have helped me and how it impacted my life. We later on regrouped and lived in one place together. We shared and helped each other. I managed our monthly budget, did the cooking for all of us and we ate together. We had our fun memories too. Some already left back home for good.

I always share this story to inspire others who are losing hope when they are in the same situation. Visa during that time was good for two months. My first visa renewal was completed in my fourth month. My second exit, which was under the hotel's name, was only used for more or less 5 days. I went back that day to the same place, and the same people I had left were still there waiting for their visas, wondering why I was back. Some of them might not be able to go back until someone will be of help. It took me, I think, only 2 days, saved by my angels in disguise. In all these worst situations, all I needed was courage, strength, strong support, and enough Faith ("to move the mountain of problems"). "And all the rest will follow".

Yes, I got the job. Unfortunately, I did not start work immediately. With a new record of debt in hand, my visa was still not processed. And I got some health issues. I was called back due to my test report and was prescribed Iron tablets, I believe my Iron improved. I stayed home and waited there was no call. The last time I followed up, I was told that I could still go on vacation, but I told them I really needed the job as soon as possible. While waiting, I was thinking of taking again a temporary job or a part-time job, but the fear of experiencing what happened at the hotel stopped me. I don't like to disappoint my would-be employer or might face stiffer consequences. And what if they call me to report? I tried to convince myself that everything would turn out right and just kept my faith above everything.

After almost two months I was called to report to work at the same hospital where I'm working until now. Truly, "patience is a virtue". If you believe and have faith, God will make wonders and will always make a way.

CHAPTER 5

The Birth of My Advocacy.

No one knows me better than myself and my family; How I was brought up? And how life was, before I got entangled with life's adversaries but I guess my friends can attest to it too. I have to go back down memory lane and maybe I could assess and understand or might find the answer how and why after all what I've been through I was and still is here surviving against all odds.

As far as I can recall, I had a normal childhood just like an ordinary kid. I grew up seeing the kindness and generosity of my parents sacrificing their own happiness for us their children and in helping other people even when life is hard. And just like them I learned along the way. I have always been a welcoming person. I can hardly say no to anyone as much as I can handle. I believe that these traits passed on to me were a combination of my dad and mom. I learned so many things from them. In real sense, I was homeschooled and I completed the course on how to live my life; I bet my siblings will say the same. They prepared us well for life. Despite all that, I still faced failures along the way, one reason why I wrote this book. No one will be spared from the harsh realities of life. We may be traversing a different road, the experiences and the way we handle and manage it may differ, but our goal will only be pointing towards the same end or purpose.

Envy is the number one enemy of peace. It will stop you from moving forward as you go along your journey. Never look at other's lives, especially your neighbours, friends or even your relatives and compare yourself. Each one has their own life to live. It's inspiring to note when one or some of them are already successful and enjoying a comfortable life with their families. Another one had a good education, now at the peak of his career, and has contributed much to society. Yes! they are really successful, very successful but one thing is sure it did not happen overnight. Success just doesn't fall down from heaven. It is a blessing but it means they did their part, they worked hard. When you look at yourself and you feel they have more, it's normal to feel bad but never take it negatively. Rejoice and be happy for them and you will find peace in your heart. I knew well because I grow up in a competitive family circle. Social norm is more acceptable. Stop pleasing others, follow your heart's desires. Instead of feeling resentful or discontented, especially when you see yourself still struggling, the best way is to stay positive. Appreciate and celebrate with them, they deserve it.

Name it, they have it all; maybe I'm exaggerating, but it's happening. Some are enjoying life abroad. They don't like to go back home, or will say, "I love my country, but this is my home now". Others say, "We will still go back home and visit once in a while, home is home". Bottomline, life is what we make it. Regardless of where, how and what we are born with, it does not define our future. We can make it big or just enough or remain as is. No one will do it for us. We have to act and conquer our battles. Learn from others who already did. Know your capabilities, talents or tools you can use. Don't sit on it. You have to act. When feeling hopeless get down on your knees and ask for guidance.

While I'm going through all of those. I almost thought of myself as a bad person and that I am being punished. That thought always disturbed me. But then I will remember friends who sought help or refuge from me. One time, I received a call from my friend whom I met through another friend, asking if she could sleepover at my place. Later, I learned that she had a misunderstanding with her husband. My place became a place of solace. I'm glad I was able to provide temporary comfort to those who need it. I was glad to know they patched up after that, and I hope they are still together these days. I haven't seen her for a long time, but she is my friend on social media. Despite my brokenness, I can still help make others whole.

The recent struggle I just went through, I was talking to my friend about how I can make out, get myself out from trouble. She helped me big time beyond her means. I used to chat and talk to her through voice calls especially in my lowest moments. Even with our time difference, she managed to entertain me. She reminded me of a common friend. A long time ago, we were younger then. They both came to tell me about what she was getting into. That other friend was so worried because they had to go as planned, so with whatever amount I had, I helped them pushed through and we joined the celebration of her wedding.

Another friend came to me looking so desperate, so I brought her home, and she was so convinced to leave her husband; I can't remember the grounds, it doesn't matter, but what should I tell her? I'm also in the same situation. It's like a blind person leading another blind. I just hope I was able to give her proper insights. I don't know if she was able to reconcile with her husband. I used to see her around, but again, I never asked. Even if they are my friends, I don't go out soliciting their stories unless they share it with me.

My friend, who is newly married, shared that her husband is still giving full support to his family. She was not jealous, I know, but she did not expect it. What she knows is that after marriage, she and her children will be the priority, and his family will come next. That was because they didn't talk about this matter from the beginning. Being the eldest and head of the family, her husband has to give full support to his siblings who are still studying until they finish school, not to mention their basic needs. The last time I talked to her, she got past that issue and have grown matured. She manages her life well now, has changed her faith, and is still working where I knew long decades ago. We are still connected through social media.

I got so many memories with friends good and bad, there is no perfect relationship. I believe there are more good things than not so good! Now that I'm not getting any younger and with so many lessons learned I only look forward to a better if not the best person I can be everywhere I go and to anyone I'm with. I may be far always from my family and my son and I hardly reach out to them but I never stop praying for their good health and safety. I still experience hardships one after the other. Relationship issues Yes! Name it, I had it too. I've been there. So many more struggles I want to share, this book will not hold it all even if I squeeze them in. But it is where I get strength and inspiration. It will not stop me from helping others in my own little ways. There will always be something we can share, even in our nothingness. That's the power of having Faith. It comes with hope, love and joy including the spirit of giving.

We all have health issues as we all have trials; they are just at different levels, degrees, and extents of seriousness. Sadly, though expected, some of my relatives and friends had gone ahead already, including those I considered closest to my heart, even though we didn't see each other much or for a long time since we grew up together during our younger years. Remembering them in my prayers. Sadness filled my heart because it meant I would no longer see them. This is the moment when we wish we should have at least made an effort to reach out to them. Visit those who are accessible despite the distance. Or at least drop by to those nearby, but we always seem to be busy with our own issues and think there is still time. Life is so vulnerable, and death is inevitable. Life is a gift with a purpose, so we should take care.

Some friends are now gone, young and old, relatives too, yours and mine. It happens anytime, anywhere and in any way which our human mind cannot understand. Mostly, we have questioned or blamed God. But we should not forget to ask ourselves, what did we do? We might get the answer that might help us to accept our fate and may lessen the pain. I always wondered, after all I'm still here. I have been to a near-death experience, too, but God let me live. Deep inside me, I know it's not by chance; it's not a choice to be made but because I still have a greater obligation to do. My life's purpose has been in my mind for a long time, but I don't know how to achieve it. It became a struggle and victory over and over again.

The exhaustive job hunting was one of my worst struggles. Three times I had to exit, expenses again, oh yes, I landed three times to Iran in Kish Island until I got my job now. Thanks God! I understand the Government why they have control over their constituents when it comes to matters of their interest because of the consequences they will both experience. Most of those who cannot find a job are either abused or neglected, will overstay and will face legal issues and more which the government will be involved.

Despite my tribulations, I never forget my spiritual obligation. I regularly go to church and joined the different community activities. Once in a while, I missed. I once promised when I get the job, I would serve more in church. I found out later that my duty timings won't allow me. I have weekend duties as well as shift duties. I broke my promise. During those early days at work, I was more focused on how to pay all my debts. I can't set my own prayer time. My mind is always disturbed. What could happen next? No clear future at all. But I did not stop going to church as much as I could. Work, home, church. I focused mostly on my work and did what I had to do. If I can do more I will do. I went beyond what was expected of me without asking anything in return. I feel more fulfilled.

Why must we go exit to renew our visit visa? It's common knowledge that for any country, there is certainly a limit for anyone not a citizen to stay or live in a particular country. At the same time, there is a limit for any of their citizens to stay out of the country. With due respect, those laws must be obeyed. Those who want to stay longer must renew their visa before it expires; otherwise, they will have to leave the country. Overstaying has an equivalent penalty. The first time I went exit to change my first visit visa, was just Airport to Airport. Me and my friend Naira together. We just stayed in the waiting area until our new visas were released, before we knew it we boarded the plane back. The second time I did, it took me more than a day. I got to share a room with different nationalities who had different stories to tell. Most of them are desperate stories, sad stories, all dreaming of a better life. And all we can do is comfort each other and give a touch of hope. There were those who were not able to go back either because they were not renewed or they had issues and just stayed. They were able to find jobs at their place of exit or were sent straight back to their own countries.

Even as years passed by, I will never forget the kind of living conditions I had to bear, the worst part was the lack of funds, though I was able to do part-time office jobs, it was not enough to sustain my needs and I also have to send to my son. With no money at hand, I had to borrow here and there, thanks God, He always works in mysterious ways and of course, my God sent saviour sister Marisa. One time, my son lost the computer he borrowed from a thief who entered his room. My mom and my sister arranged for a replacement. In every struggle and every experience, I'm also collecting knowledge, wisdom and inspiration to help myself and keep going. Friends come and go, but I make sure that my encounter with them will not go in vain. I learn from them, and they learn from me. As Much as I can, I will help. My life principle is, to go the extra mile in everything I do without expecting something in return. And to always pay forward as

I move forward.

On a lighter note, in all of these experiences, my struggles were not like others; I was not lucky enough, and I did not find my knight in shining armour to save the damsel in distress or the lucky charm to bring me to success. Nevertheless, I pulled it through. It took time, though, but it's worth the lessons I learned. And for women out there, be careful not to be swayed by empty words and promises, especially when your heart is involved. It's not bad to dream of success but don't allow yourself to be manipulated. For most expatriates, the dream to change the course of their lives is very strong, especially to be out of poverty. There are so many ways, but usually, the easy way is not the best. It is temporary, it will not last long, or it can make matters worse rather than solve it. I'm no different in my struggles. I was tempted many times. I have been in situations where it is easy to give up. I met people who chose a different path. People who caused others misfortune, leading others to go astray. There are those who like to give unsolicited advice that sometimes helpful but mostly not at all. Everyone has a point of view, and we all differ in our ideas, principles, strategies, and beliefs. There are others who seem to be perfectly right when talking, but it's different when managing their own lives. How will you react, and to whom you listen? Well, see the truth in the way they live their lives.

When faced with uncertainties, remember to always go back. Take a review of your own past, the good things and the bad, the joys and the sorrows and take it from there. Think again of your dreams, your family or for whom you are doing it for. There is hope. It's not too late to start all over again and follow a better path. I have had bad choices. I made mistakes. I hurt my loved ones. I acted out of heightened emotions and made selfish decisions. And this is because of our human weaknesses. It's a natural reaction for us. But we can do better than that if we examine ourselves. When dealing with others in any situation, give yourself time to think. I want to share what I learned from my Christian Formation Conference. In everything we do, we need to understand and discern before we decide. Please THINK!

T-is it True

H-is it Helpful

I-is it Inspiring

N-is it Necessary

K-is it Kind

After every trial I went through, I realized that those were the best times to give a moment to myself. A time to slow down and ponder or meditate. A time to grieve during a time of loss or a time to heal during a time of illness or weakness. It will not be the same for all as the experiences and way of living are different from each other. We can see that the lives of others are better than those of us, but we can be better than others, too. If we are feeling bad for ourselves, what about those who are suffering more than us? We often feel left out because we see how others are enjoying their lives while we are struggling. When this happens to me, I always go back. And it will confront me point blank. It is all about me. Not about my family. But I'm happy, and I know I'm blessed that my family is doing well. People I met brought stories of their family or relatives who are doing better, who are well off, who are successful, and they become proud of them. But at the end of the day, it is not our family's accomplishments that matter, but yours or mine.

Every time I reached a crossroad, felt confused or face a dead end, where normally human nature would immediately feel defeated, I have to remind myself I'm not alone. We have faith that will keep bringing us to the light after every darkness. It's not easy I know to say that in every struggle, there is always good thing that will happen. Do not look at the dark side of every situation, hidden by the pains. This will push us to think of the easiest way to escape from it. And if we will not be able to weigh things out because we are clouded by emotions, like anger, or you're feeling exhausted, and it seems the world is going against you. The Temptation to go astray when you are at your lowest moment is very strong, you have to guard your emotions. This is where empty promises, personal interest, self-centeredness and greed from other people come in, and unknowingly, you give them signals out of hopelessness and will take advantage of the situation. Otherwise, you will feel defeated and you feel self-pity, and you will blame yourself. Sometimes, giving up can be a solution or can bring healing to those affected, but you still want to go on because no matter how bad it is, you still see a ray of hope in it. But you can't do it alone, and so in all of these, it is very clear that without help, this can break you down; you will lose everything, your hard work and even your loved ones, and if not addressed immediately, you will lose yourself and will lead you to depression.

Sadly, nowadays, troubles can be caused by other people we don't even know or meet in person but through social media. We used to hear that the tongue is the most powerful weapon; it can destroy a person, but it can be a medium used to obtain peace. Now, it's a click of a finger away. It can change one's life for the better, and worse, it can destroy it. We are all created perfectly with a beautiful soul inside and out. Wherever we are, whatever we may, it's just right to be grateful for the life given to us by free. It's best to use it, share it and be our Creator's living witness. Again, our life is a gift given to us not for our own personal gain but with God's purpose. Through our lives, we can also give life. A simple smile can warm the heart of one sad soul. "It's better to be kind than to be right".

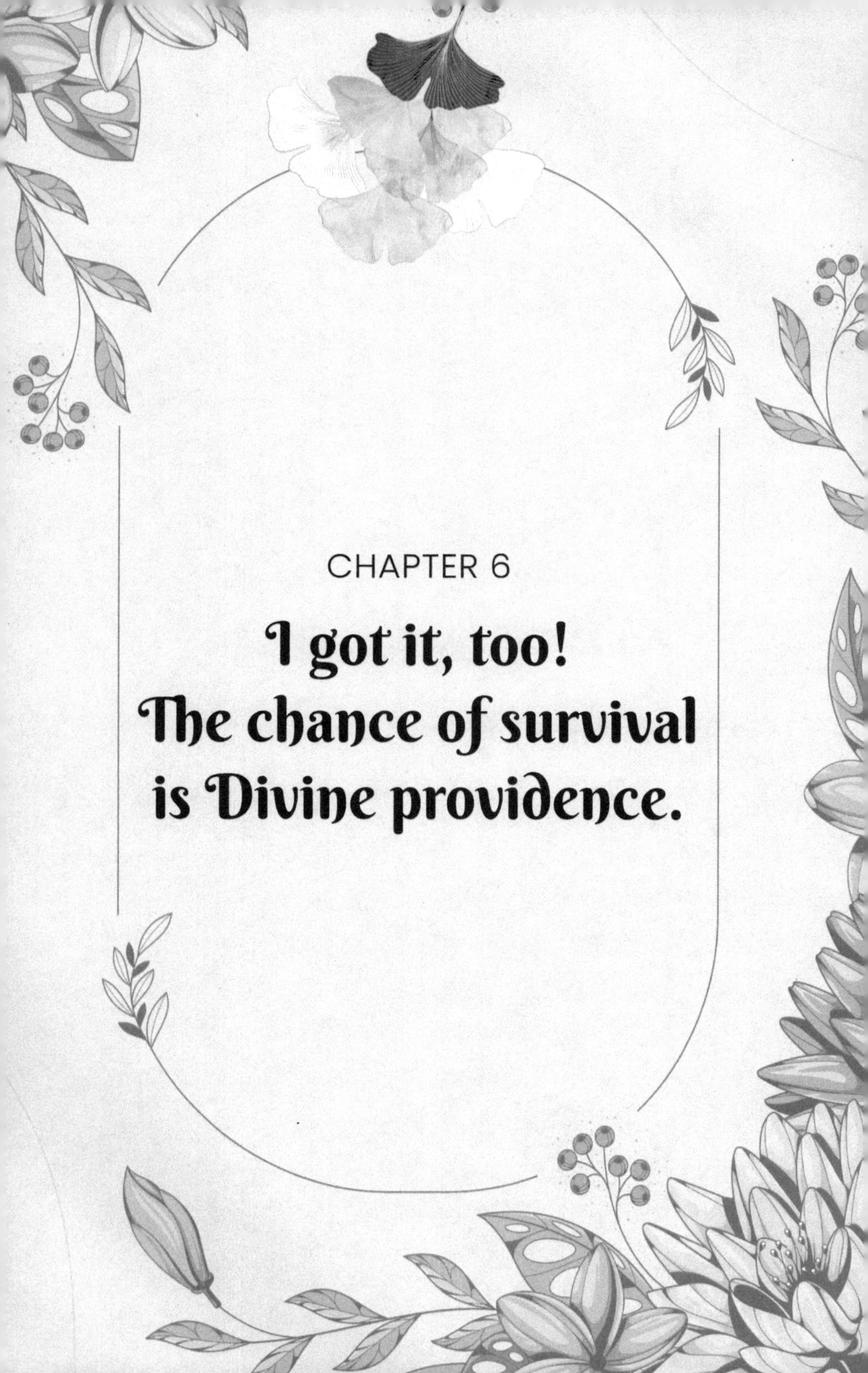

CHAPTER 6

I got it, too!
The chance of survival
is Divine providence.

Part 1 – When I was diagnosed

"In memory of all my friends and relatives who triumphed in their battles but left ahead of us. They are now singing with the choirs of angels in heaven."

Fast forward from my joining work in 2007 to August of 2011, I was diagnosed with Stage 3 Breast Cancer. Two months earlier, I just came from vacation back home in the Philippines. It was fun, filled with family bonding escapades and overflowing joy and laughter. Meeting old friends and going to places. Making up for the lost time. I never saw it coming. We had lots of fun and were full of wonderful experiences, but a month is not enough. Before we knew it, we were bidding goodbyes at home, giving our big hugs to everyone, wishing each other well and off we went to our separate destinations. No one knows if we will ever see each other again.

But the week before leaving, suddenly I got heavy bleeding, so I hid the advice of my cousin, a Gynaecologist, Dra. Joyce. Two days before my flight, I did the D & C procedure and cleared any suspicions of abnormality before my flight.

Three years earlier, I had an unexplained bleeding condition, and I did a thorough checkup at my workplace, Women and Children's Hospital; after some tests and consultations, it was dismissed as a premenopausal stage. I was 39 years old. I took some medications and went on with my normal routine. Shortly after that, during one of my night shifts, I noticed I was having blurry vision, and I almost slipped down the stairs. It prompted me to do a blood test before the end of my shift. My haemoglobin dropped as low as 6g/dl (Normal value for females: 12.1 - 15.1g/dl sometimes varies on the test they used). I needed an emergency blood transfusion, I received three bags, to be exact; it somehow helped to increase my blood count but remained at the lowest range. But I was feeling better.

When we reached the Airport, it was raining heavily, my flight was cancelled and delayed for 2 days. I was on a connecting flight. I stayed another 2 days in Brunei, enough for me to have a good rest after the procedure and the long days of travel. As soon as I joined back to work, I immediately made an appointment with the gynaecologists to follow up on my health issue. She told me her own findings and asked me to repeat them for confirmation. Because of my high cholesterol level, I have maintenance, but she prescribed other medicines which I did not take because I realized the pricking pains I felt was on the right side, far from my heart.

Then came Ramadan. It is the Holy month of fasting, prayer and good deeds. Work is shortened, this is the time where we can have some moments with ourselves. At one point during that time, I accidentally felt a small lump on my upper right chest, exactly where I was feeling frequent pricking pains.

Initially, I felt something was there, but my denying self said it was nothing. The next day, I woke up and touched it again, maybe it was not there, oh! No, it's still there! Faced with the "what if" question, I said, "what if not," and again brushed it off. I was praying, but I felt more disturbed. At first, I kept it to myself, then later on, I told my friends, Kawkab (Jordan) and Ulfat (Yemen), during an Iftar meal at Kawkab's house. I'm always invited and welcomed as a member of their family. Same with Ulfat. Both are my friends of different nationalities who always made me feel loved to the core. No holds barred when we are together. I followed their advice. Most of the time, I always live alone and on my own, at the end of the day, I always follow what is at my convenience. If I'm the one, I can delay it until eternity, and worst of all, it will be too late. Obviously, I was hesitant, but happily, I obliged it was for my sake.

It was my friend Ulfat who made an appointment with the Staff clinic Physician. I informed her about my concern. I just felt some frequent pricking pains in my upper right chest, ignorable though, I can just brush it off, but I also just realized I have been having a feeling of numbness in my right arm for a very long time, but I put the blame on my shoulder bag. The Physician did not examine me, but she told me because of the lump and my age, she would refer me to the Radiology department and do the mammogram in a different hospital related to my workplace. I went on the day of my appointment.

I knew it already when the technician told me to meet with the radiologist. After the mammogram, she called me to the ultrasound room. I could sense the way she was rolling the probe left and right longer than expected and kept asking me questions like trying to rule out any possibility that would not lead to what was already obvious to her. With urgency, she gave me the instruction to go to the breast clinic at the other hospital linked to my workplace and meet a certain surgeon because that very same day was his clinic day, and if I miss, I need to wait for another week. Not only that, she personally contacted the doctor to arrange for him to take me as a walk-in patient. It's not a usual thing for a busy Physician like her to do it, but she made sure that I would go, and she gave me the Surgeon's contact number to follow up.

I'm already feeling anxious. She told me that I might do a biopsy. Perplexed, I forgot that doing a biopsy requires preparation, so it will not happen on the same day. There were so many things going on in my mind at that time, but I don't know what exactly. My whole being is in trance and my mind is already focused on the biopsy thing. I've been on my own for quite a long time now and I have always been strong, certified, tried and tested. That time at that very moment, yes, I was still composed; in my right senses, I could still say, it's fine; I can do it another day. I will just go back to work, but in reality, my world stopped. Maybe for an hour, a minute or a split second. But it literally stopped.

Part 2 - The Procedures and Preparation for Treatment

I decided to call the Surgeon for one last time. He picked up my call, and I was so nervous because I didn't know what to tell him. Obviously, he got first-hand information, so he also gave me instructions to meet him in his clinic and do the registration as a walk-in patient so I would be accommodated. True enough, he managed to meet me, but only after he was done with all those who were already on his list of patients that day. I was the last patient and he did not mind extending his duty.

Our hospital system was interlinked. He opened my file and took some time to study my reports. I was lucky; my friend Kawkab had an appointment in the same hospital. She came over, and we both met the Surgeon. My surgeon is a very kind and soft-spoken local middle-aged guy. In Arabic, he was able to explain my condition to Kawkab and, alternately, in English to me but without confirming it yet. He convinced me that we still need more tests and some procedures to be done before he will come to the correct diagnosis. He gave me all the appointments I needed and waited for each to be done. Some of them are CT scans, MRIs, bone scans, and more. I went home that evening still blank, but I also don't like to jump to conclusions like my surgeon. I did not tell anyone.

I went to work as normal as possible until the end of the week; while waiting for my transport, I happened to mention to a nurse colleague that I had done some tests, but I don't know the reports yet. Then she reminded me I could open my file and check it in the system. Suddenly, I wanted to run back inside, but the excitement of seeing my reports immediately faded away because there was no time left. I was just waiting for some staff, and we would move. I did not think of that at work, maybe because my mind was preoccupied, and I still didn't want others to know about it. That was Thursday when our week started from Sunday to Thursday; the next day, Friday, was weekend, and it was my day off.

Saturday came, I was morning shift, the anxious waiting was over and off I went to work. I could have called and asked any of my colleagues to open my file, but I wanted to be the first one to know about it. They still don't know yet what I'm going through. I reached the hospital and there I just saw that my friend Kawkab was on night shift. She was actually preparing to leave once the morning shift arrived. As soon as I approached her, I asked her to open my file, I gave my Medical Record no. I told her to open it, and she assured me, "Don't worry, mama, everything will be alright" I really miss her with Baba Waleed and Farah. They migrated to the US. We call each other mama, and Arab mothers often use it when talking to their son or daughter, like a magic word showing their strong affection.

While she was opening my file, I went to her back to peek at the screen, and there we saw the initial diagnosis from the mammogram and the ultrasound reports. There you are, the glaring, deafening reality. As soon as I saw the words Breast CA (Right Breast), I could feel the struggling voice of Kawkab controlling her tears trying to say something while I blurted out with a smile, I knew it. I actually felt that tears wanted to flow from my eyes, but nothing came out. I felt numb at that time, we couldn't both exchange words. I just saw her pick up her bag, and while walking away, she said something like take care, don't think too much until she disappeared from my sight.

Though I was ready to accept my fate, it took time to sink in. It's "Invasive Ductal Carcinoma, Grade II". Later on, I confirmed with one of our Oncologists that it was already Stage 3. Looking back, it was actually a simple term because nowadays, I get to hear so many types of complex terms, but in layman's term, it all just plainly means Breast CA. And this is because the disease is advancing, becoming more complex. It is rapidly developing on its own.

Thanks God, I became busy with patients, I can't even remember how I passed the day, no time to reflect or even think about what I discovered that morning. No one to talk to except for the patients who are coming one after the other. The day ended and I went home. It was a shared flat, I only had the four corners of my own room to hear me. Thinking of sharing it early with my flatmates was not yet an option. After I will confirm with the biopsy then I will make the announcement. It took me almost a month to complete all the procedures because there were issues that came up in between. Slowly, the news spread and literally I asked and solicited prayers for my healing from anyone who I knew and who knew me at work, in church, and in some groups and organizations I joined.

At some point, I took the courage to tell my brother, Rommel, by text. While I was sending messages, he was calling and I'm cutting him off because I want first to tell him all the information but I still don't know what to tell him. I can only remember that I assured him I was doing fine and strictly told him not to inform our family until I got confirmation from my attending physician, who still was not willing to give me a clear answer. I first told him that after all the procedures before the biopsy, maybe I would be ready to tell them. But still, I couldn't. My brother stood by my side when I needed him most. He went beyond to lend me a helping hand despite his work timings.

My attending physician called me back again, to inform me that as per the MRI, they saw a highly suspicious mass in my left breast not seen through the ultrasound. We couldn't proceed to do the biopsy because they didn't have an MRI-assisted biopsy. He told me to talk to the radiologist and ask for her opinion. She informed me that since the exact location is not determined, they can only do multiple pricks and collect as many samples as they can nearest to the supposed target location that they can't actually pinpoint. I went home thinking of the struggle I would be going through. As I was slowly coming back to my senses, not that I lost it, but the truth is I was feeling relieved, slowly understanding and appreciating this one kind of bumpy ride. The journey was so unexpected that I learned to deal with it day by day as it comes, no longer as a threat or something that I should be scared from but I was embracing it the best possible way I can in a positive note.

I already know that worrying will not make a difference. Collecting all my thoughts after all the frequent travel to and from my medical procedure appointments and in between my work, including the power of prayers from all those who are praying for me, I felt I was especially blessed in one way or another. I began to feel at peace with my situation and my health.

In the middle of all the chaos it initially created in my mind, I went home one day, sat in front of my altar and cried my heart out. I did not ask God, why me? His answer may be, why not? Because obviously there can be 1001 chances that indirectly I may have caused it. I did not pray to make promises to be better if I get healed. I did not blame nor curse God for all these misfortunes happening in my life. Instead, I poured out all the negativity out of my system. I asked God for forgiveness in all aspects of my life, including not taking care of my health because I still didn't get over my unhealthy eating habits. I prayed, "If it is Your will that I be given a chance to live longer, make me a living witness of your goodness and glory! But if it means the end of my journey on this earth, then so be it. I will gladly accept it. Amen"

When the Dr called me, I had already made the decision to undergo a double mastectomy (which means removing both breasts). I did a biopsy only on my right breast to finally confirm the diagnosis from what the previous tests and procedures have already reported and identify the extent and the probable cause and effect of the affected area. The left breast after mastectomy. The biopsy confirmed the diagnosis; I must have surgery immediately before I can start the treatment.

It was just after my biopsy that I had the courage to initiate the video call to my sister Marisa, she is an oncology nurse. My brother, true to his word, did not leak out the information until I was ready; I was in constant contact with him, though, for updates. And at one time or another, he took his time out to check on me. I contacted my sister through Skype, which was the means of communication at that time. I first sent her the reports through email before the video call, so I told her to open it up, and while she was reading, I was watching her. She was in tears and while talking she was immediately preparing a plan in her mind. Whatever happened, I already accepted my fate and surrendered my life. Seeing her in tears just reminded me how I am truly loved. I showed her I was doing fine. With all smiles, I was calmly talking to her because I was already at peace and had come to terms with my condition. The day before that, I attended the CFC HOLD National Conference, and I poured out all my worries and pains to the Lord.

Then she passed on the camera to dad I got the chance to talk personally inform him; we reassured each other of the love of God, and everything would turn out right. He told me the usual words of a caring father. I remember when me and my siblings were younger and one of us would be late coming home, he would do his roll call and say, "even the chicks with the mother Hen we have to make sure they are home before dark", he is always right. My mom was at work. I appreciated very much how hardworking my parents were. At their old age, they still managed to work at a facility to take care for the aged in the US, actually some younger than them. They stopped working when they had their grandchildren to care. The same as they did with my son and my other siblings' children back home. The human epitome of God's love and care.

I asked them not to inform yet my son, John Marc, because I didn't know how he would react or might be affected with the situation. I thought I needed to prepare him for the worst. My sister Marisa went on to arrange to fly Dad and Mom alternately to take care of me after surgery and on to my chemotherapy. My first scheduled surgery was postponed, but that day, I was so grateful that one nurse colleague came by to pray the Holy Rosary with me. Then, after all the hassles and postponements, finally, my surgery went well on October 19, 2011.

True enough, I got company. Dad showed up at the hospital a few days after my surgery and stayed for a month until I recovered. It was all good for me until the time of the dreaded chemotherapy came into play. During my good moments, we showed Dad around some of Dubai's tourist attractions. Dad was with me during my first chemotherapy. An unforgettable experience of pain and indescribable feelings. Because as soon as the chemo drug entered my veins, my world totally changed, I felt weak and just stared blankly at the ceiling. Dad was there to hold my hand as my fingers felt severe pain and with headache and nausea all at the same time. Overall I passed my first taste of what a chemotherapy means. With my brother, they brought me home. I was literally lying in bed, still feeling drugged and weak until the next day when Dad together with my brother and family came by and brought as dinner. Then dad had to say his prayers and good bye and left back to the US.

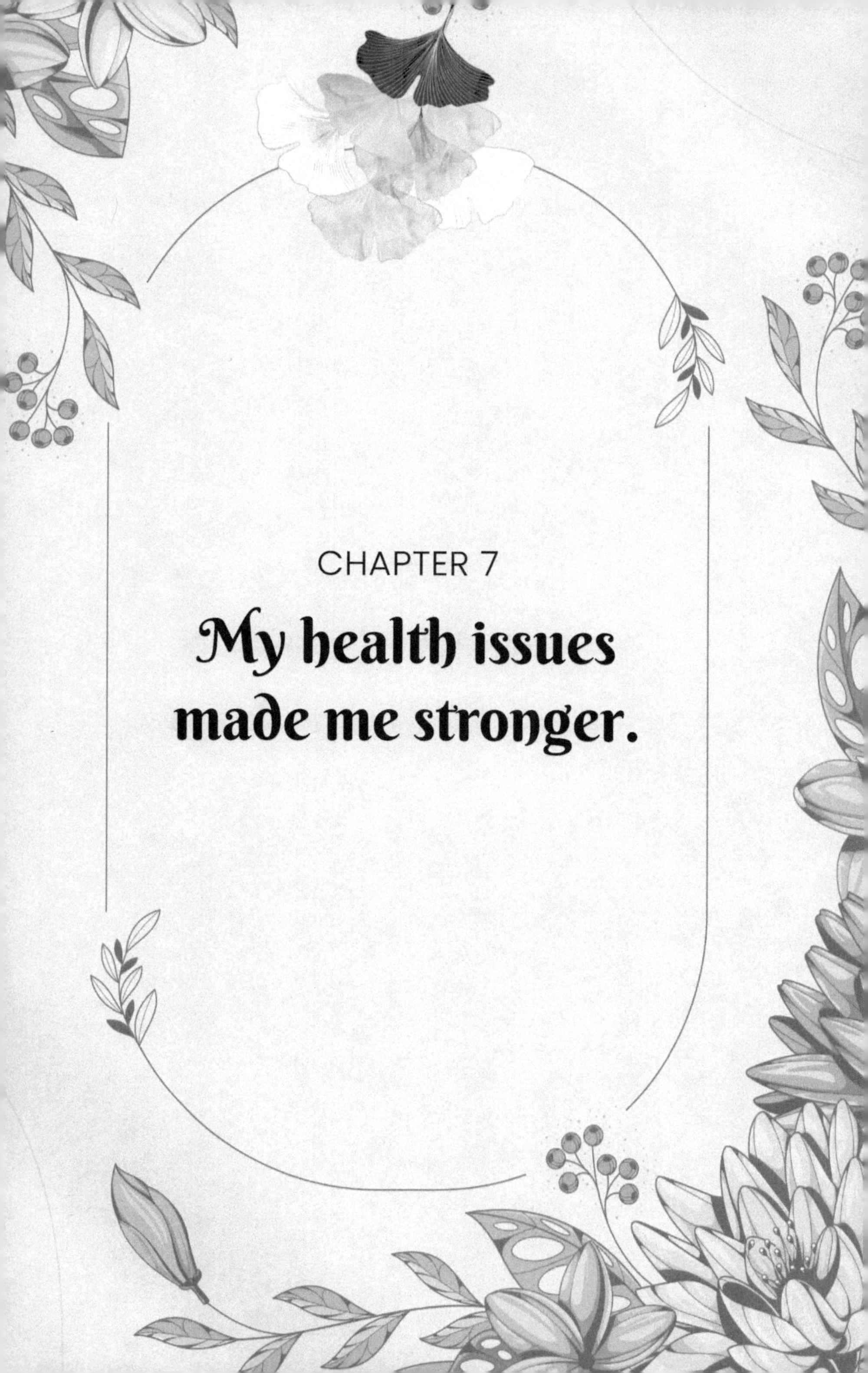

CHAPTER 7

My health issues made me stronger.

decided to talk about my Treatment separately. So many realizations happened during that time. Love, care and support surprisingly abound from everywhere. I received kindness and unending goodness from other people, prayers, and generosity, even from people whom I barely know. And most of all, the undying support of my family, my dad and mom who came to be with me and my son, who is the only reason why I want to live longer and continue to fight until God willed me to live. Surgery though scary, it's another reason to be grateful for God's mercy and the grace of skills. My experience was a smooth, carefully executed, successful procedure. Next to God, I am thankful to my surgeon, who is truly a very kind and caring man and his team. I did not have many complaints of pain or feeling of discomfort. It all went well. The next thing I knew, I immediately requested the nurse, still wondering, that I needed a full bath. From the time of my diagnosis, I was already informed that not only would I go through Chemotherapy, but I still needed to undergo Radiation. Aggressive as it sounds. This everyone should know. Early detection has a higher possibility of being treated and healed. And lesser expenses.

Before I was diagnosed, I was supporting communities and organizations that campaign and help for the early detection and immediate diagnosis of all forms of cancer or illnesses. I used to join the "Pink Walkathon" and all sorts of walks for a cause, concerts for a cause and as much as I can donate for a cause. One year before, I joined a known group for a cause, and I walked for a member of our church community and some other friends of friends and unknowns, who might be a sick relative or people I know but I'm not aware of. Later on, I learned I do have, sadly they later succumb to their illnesses; God bless their souls. The following year, I failed to join the "Walk", but my friends walked for me, not in my place but as one of their "causes." The succeeding walks, while still recovering, I joined again and brought with me some of my friends. One time, I was with my ever-supportive sister, Ruby Joy and my friend Kawkab's daughter, Farah. I called her my little big sister. She was a small girl then, but like her mom, she did a lot for me, too, even accompanying me to church.

Chemotherapy, for me, was tougher than surgery, though I carry with me my scars as a survival trophy; I saw fellow patients suffer during the process and heard some gross and painful stories. But in my case, I can remember the worst pain only during the first time, when I was with my dad then the others we had fun. We were together for almost a month while I recuperated from the surgery. When I got the schedule of my first treatment, just like my surgery, it was postponed because my Oncologist just realized that it needs at least a month to heal after surgery before treatment. My sister Ruby Joy and my husband Andrew came by to visit so I jumped out of bed literally and from the hospital straight we took the metro train, the most accessible mode of transportation. We took Dad around the City to eat and visit some places. He did like it, found this place amazing and all the people he met and wished to come back again. I wish I could still bring him back here.

So many people other than those I already mentioned, I want to extend my great thanks, May God grant you a hundredfold of overflowing blessings. When my diagnosis was finally confirmed by my surgeon, I was already prepared to start my journey. No worries, no stress. I surrendered all up to the Lord Almighty and I'm ready to let the world know. I'm going on an uncertain road trip, and I'm not sure where it's going and when I will be coming back, but it's no longer necessary to know. I'm ready and everything is under control. Then, I started opening up to everyone. Other than my friends who knew earlier, I informed my colleagues, most of my friends, churchmates, and actually anyone I met. As long as there is a chance to talk about it, I just literally bring it out. One day, I called Janet and met with her to tell her my story. Not long before, she decided to move in and become my hand help from cooking to washing to cleaning until Mom came. It was Divine providence I met my cousin Janet earlier. I didn't know she was also here, along with her sister. In another time, we met with other relatives who often come to visit me during my ordeal, too. Shirley and husband Mike, and their kids, and there was Rono and his family, who took me as Godmother during his adult baptism at St. Mary's Catholic Church, Dubai. There were so many I met, especially in the different organizations and small communities, that all became part of my journey. Thank you is never enough.

And to my flatmates during that time, who shared their flat with me. They are one family related to each other and a friend. We are of different faith but it was never an issue. It was my 4th home when I joined them. But we shifted again, my 5th home when I got diagnosed. Yes, Thank God! I gradually progressed from living conditions in old villas to flats in different areas from Dubai to Sharjah. I was still with them during my treatment and they were supportive even when my cousin Janet and my mom stayed with us. They understood what I'd been going through, and they were with me until I was back to almost normal. Most of the time, I was not feeling well, and I struggled to walk, especially after every procedure. But even alone, I did my best to attend the daily evening masses at church, especially the Sundays of obligation (Anticipated Sunday Holy masses are also celebrated on a Friday & Saturday to accommodate all those who have different days off. Now on Saturday's only).

My son JM came to know about my condition. After my surgery, my cousin Bertha, who was taking care of my nephew Nathan at that time, became my instant caregiver at the hospital. Dad was with me during the day and Bertha during the night. I asked Bertha to set up a video call with JM on my bed; they are good friends. Camera facing her, she told JM she was sick, and that's why she was in the hospital. While they were talking, I joined them, and I was surprised he already knew it. He sensed something was going on, so he followed me on social media by reading the comments on my page. Even though I tried to keep it a secret, it still came out. He became curious about the words flooding my profile, especially the words "get well soon" and the prayers and well wishes. I was relieved to know that he took my condition lightly, and he was also positive that I was okay. He had always known he has a strong mom with a positive attitude, and he felt good about it. There was one time he wrote to me, he called me his "hero." I still have all his letters to me. I collected them since he wrote to me the first time.

When he learned that his grandparents (arranged by my sister) would come one after the other to be with me during my ordeal, he also asked how about him. I did give it a second thought. I was on sick leave, although still receiving my regular salary, but I still had to pay my utility bills, rent and credit cards. I had no extra budget, but I knew we have to see each other, I had to find a way. No one knows what will happen next and by God's grace, I was able to bring him just after Dad left for the US. For a very short time, we did have good times together, but I felt sorry we had to survive with whatever I had. He stayed for only two weeks. I guess it was his third visit, but this time, it was not for fun and pleasure but to take care of his sick mommy. He assisted me in a few of my treatments and frequent visits with my oncologist. Then it's supposed to be mom's turn to come. We were supposed to fetch her at the airport. Jm will meet Mom at least before he leaves. But my sister had to move mom's flight. She suddenly got a fever. Her Dr suggested taking medications first as a precautionary measure because she will come to take care of me and it will not do me good if I catch any virus.

My son left as scheduled because summer classes had begun, and he was already behind. Mom came only after a week. I remember John Marc's father told him it was okay to miss school and stay with me since he was already here, the school started and they might not allow him to join. My son panicked because he should not miss those subjects or else it would delay his studies. I had to argue and get some help from friends from the university working there, aside from his father. I did reach out to my super nice good friend and classmate in college, but not at the College of Law, Atty. Cheryl, she is holding a good position in the government; her assignment is in Geneva, Switzerland. Grateful for her help, my son was accepted. The school just asked for supporting documents.

At the airport, again Mom was delayed because I didn't know I had to send her copy of visit visa. Thanks to the good Samaritan who lent his mobile, my mom was able to contact me. It's late, but I was able to sort it out. Thankful to Jema, my flatmate, who accompanied me and patiently waited. Most of all, thank you, Lord God, for giving me my parents. At their old age, they came to take care of me. Mom was not new to the UAE. Years earlier, my sister-in-law Kat brought her and Nathan for the first time, so she saw more places than Dad. She brought so many things that my sister sent with her. Dad earlier brought California apples and oranges and some other delicacies too, that the nurses and those who came to visit me enjoyed in my hospital room.

MY mom patiently stayed with me only in my room and went out only during my treatments. It was at this moment that I got time not only to have a good rest but also to have real-time for myself after a long time. I had what I called my "sick moments" and "well moments." When I feel sick, just like after treatment, I just lie down in bed, and we watch movies or TV news from back home. When I'm well, we go to church and, once in a while, go walking in the park. I was avoiding crowded places then. And it helped me a lot to recuperate fast. Mom took care of me for three months in just the four corners of my room.

I had 16 cycles, 4 of them every three weeks, which was the hardest, and the last 12, once every week. I thought it will still be tough, so I agreed for another surgery to put a porta catheter on my chest for the succeeding treatments. I had body pains and unto my knees. I can't get down to kneel, sit and stand without pain, and I can't even walk properly. My hand (only the left hand was used for cannula and blood collection) was so painful, weak and I can't stretch anymore. That's why it's so hard for me to get back to work in between treatments and travelling to visit the Dr for my appointments other than my chemotherapy I was exhausted.

The 1st of the 16 cycles and the 1st of the strong ones. With no expectations, no idea at all, like a real warrior ready for the battle of her life. I went with Dad to the hospital with full smiles, chatting with the other patients and the nurses while taking pictures, I might use them someday. Everything was fine, so I thought. But after the treatment, I became silent, and I can't explain the feeling of the first time. I thought one day, to fulfil one of my dreams, I will write a documentary about it.

After the Dr gave the overview of my whole treatment, I was given the dosage of the pre-chemo drugs (has to be given first every treatment), next the chemo drugs. As soon as the chemo drug was pushed into my veins, I started to feel the terrible pain in my finger nearest to the cannula. I learned later on that the flow can be reduced, and so can the pain, but I tolerated it. I was not aware. I thought that's what is it. Suddenly, my migraine sets in then my period. All I know is that I felt weakened, couldn't move and was too lazy to talk. One patient came by my bed to check on me and cheer me up before she left. She noticed I became silent and not as active as when I came in.

After my next 2nd chemo, I started losing my hair. I asked my cousin Janet to cut and actually shave my head because the burning feeling in my scalp caused me terrible headache. I look beautiful without hair. Three months later, my period stopped. I also began to notice physical changes as well as constant pains everywhere. Eight months of needles and drugs, as well as restricted movements, ended well. During those treatments, mom has to get up early to boil the eggs that we will bring for my breakfast so we will not buy anymore. My treatment routine included going up to the canteen to buy boiled eggs and slices of bread with syrup and jam. I can't eat other food for breakfast.

But that's not all. My body took a month's break after chemotherapy before I underwent radiation. Again, it was postponed. The Dr learned I still had my porta catheter. He suggested removing it (again by surgery) because radiation will pass through the area. My oncologist told me to keep it for at least 2 years more in case I will need it. I went back and had it removed. I believed I didn't need it anymore.

Mom was supposed to extend her stay so I could have company during my radiation. We were still deciding to renew her visa, which will expire in a few days. We dropped by my sister Ruby Joy's place near the area. From there, I felt for Mom; she had gone through so much already and had done much more to take care of me. One time, her BP went up, and it got me worried; I had her checked and was given medication. Besides, I can already take care of myself, and I will be near my sister, who I can also stay with on weekends. I went back with Mom to remove my porta catheter until I recovered. We decided not to renew her visa. We sent her off to the airport before I head back for my radiation. I'm forever grateful to my sister's generosity, my parents' spirit of sacrifice, and my whole family's prayers for me.

I had radiation for almost a month. I made new friends. We are four, and we got along well, especially since we have the same case and the same story to share. We support each other. We had separate rooms, but we cooked, ate together and had fun mostly in my room. These were all for free, we only brought our personal things and food. We also have free transportation, pick and drop from the accommodation to the hospital. It was roughly 15 minutes of treatment each day, and the remaining time was spent together. There was a room for some activity to relax. We did paintings and some handicrafts, which I enjoyed doing, and I made a lot of it all for the centre. We parted ways but were in contact. Sadly, though, we lost one of us, it was pandemic time, we cannot travel to pay our final respect. I remember we attended her wedding a few years after we finished our treatment together, but for her, it came back to her bones. She had treatment but succumbed to it one year later.

Every weekend, I spent time with my sister Joy because they lived in the same area. She made so many sacrifices for me, taking care of me while we were together. She and Andrew worked in different hospitals. They too had passed through trials and God healed them both until they were blessed with their daughter, AJ. They left for Canada, where they now reside and had another baby Kovi. It was during those times that, despite my sickness, my brokenness, my emptiness and feeling alone, I got overwhelming support. All throughout that journey, I was never really alone. My family all came aboard and joined me on the trip of a lifetime. My parents, in their old age, braved their way, travelling miles away to witness their daughter fight her battle while they themselves were in pain because of the uncertainty of my situation. Only God knows if I will survive. Everyone were my prayer warriors, and with that, we all trusted, hoped and patiently believed in God's promise, "Be not afraid; I am with you until the end of time". And true enough, God, true to His promises, gave back my health and normal life even my Dr told me I'm no longer normal. It took time, but I survived. It's only by the grace of God.

Humans, by nature are never satisfied. We tend to ask for more and more. We have to know there's an end to everything. Enough is enough we cannot take more than our capacity. And we have to accept that not everything we wish for we will have. No matter what happens, always look at the bright side of life instead of feeling hopeless. We have to accept our human weaknesses and remain positive. Stay focused and surrender everything to the Almighty. Trust in God's providence, whatever it is, His will be done.

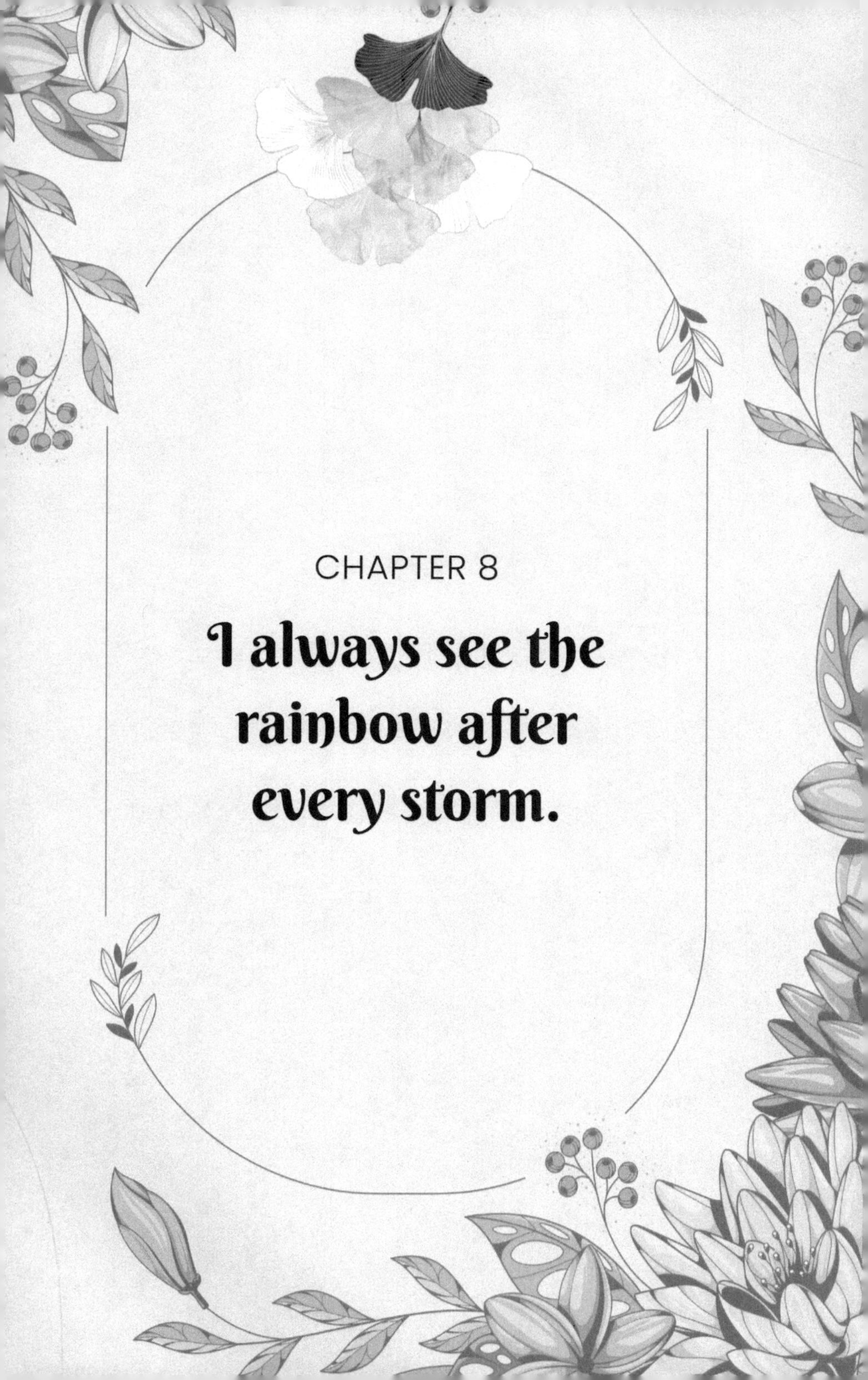

CHAPTER 8

I always see the
rainbow after
every storm.

Seventeen years ago, on January 13, 2007, was my first day at work. I hopped from one house to another, sharing the room as bed space until I was able to afford my own room and later my own flat. Going through those experiences all over in my mind is very exhausting. Truly life is tough. But I can say it's a bed of roses but full of thorns.

The reason why I had a blood transfusion just a few months after I newly joined work was that I was diagnosed with severe iron deficiency anaemia. I mentioned earlier that before I joined work, I had to go back to repeat my blood test a week after I was given Iron tablets. That means my iron deficiency persisted all the while. Again, I had to take medications but free of charge. I was sure the reason was due to my earlier poor living conditions. Also, psychologically, I was anxious every day about "how long will I be able to find a job or will I be able to find one?" for not having a regular meal or a healthy eating habit and, most especially, being deprived of having enough and good sound sleep. But as always, God is good! I recovered fast and got back to work stronger. Then, my unexplained heavy period was presumed to be an early menopausal stage, so I was prescribed hormone treatment. But it was later correlated by my surgeon as the onset of my breast cancer that was only detected two years later. Despite my health conditions and living alone, I continued working. I love my job and am so inspired that I can do more than what is expected without asking in return. My colleagues thought it was a show. I heard them say they were hoping I would not change. But until now, I've still been doing what I do. I believe I made a point and I have proven whether everyone agrees with me or not.

We can never avoid envy or personal interest not to get in between working relationships, I was a victim to it but I was able to show them that I work not to glorify myself but to do it for the spirit of service. I care for the institution I worked for. I make sure to perform well and contribute in my own little ways, but most especially, I always think of what is best for the customer, the best service I can give to the beneficiary of my service. Work must be done correctly and completely. Not overdone or worst underdone. It should not only be based on the benefit received in return, but it must be accomplished with a heart. If you put your heart into and finish a job, you yourself will feel satisfied. You will attract positivity and good things will freely flow. More than that, they know me because I share everything, not only my time and my strength but also a little of my meagre salary. I even go beyond what I can afford just so I can help.

My life principle is always that in everything I do, I go the extra mile. I was strong and active then, but I always had reservations. I only act when I am involved, if I have reason to interfere or if I am asked to, but I will always give my all. I never leave work undone. I will not leave any stone unturned until I solve an issue. Most of the time, I'm misinterpreted. I can't argue, but in the kind of world we live in, the reaction depends on situation, condition and worst emotions of the one involved. Anyone doing their best becomes an enemy and will cause division. Experiences or past events can dictate how we interpret matters in front of us, and we perceive them as the same rather than using our critical thinking and proper reasoning to deal with them properly. In my personal experience, some fix their gaze on the incentives or wait for promotion before they will lift a finger. It's sad because that's the reality, I understand that each one has the responsibility to fulfil needs that are not even covered. It causes one to lose interest and will just go on wanting more but their work is half done. But it's not right.

It took me almost a year from diagnosis to treatment. I can go back to work and slowly do some things I can handle. After all, I was not really helpless. I can still go to church and walk in the park. One funny story, during one of my chemo sessions, one Dr who is one with us, a CA patient too, told me in front of my son, "I like your attitude and the way you smile and take things lightly". It will help you heal fast, so keep that positive disposition. The medicines they are giving us, she said, has actually no effect if we stop living. You exude positive energy that helps in the healing process. Go out and enjoy!" That evening, my son told me he wanted to go out at least to the mall and I said I don't feel like going out. And he said you heard the Dr what she said; "so let's better go out and enjoy " I can't forget that Dr I hope and pray that she made it too. I met her once. I didn't get her name, but her words made an impact on me. But my heavy feeling from my chemo session that day won over my desire to go out with my son. I wish I did. It happened again, I felt bad because my son was disappointed. He wanted so much to watch a movie and pleaded with me to be with him inside, but it was not safe for me, so I waited outside. My son just wanted to catch up but I'm not always able to.

He came back again five years later just after I undergone, TAHBSO, an elective surgery as a precaution. Actually, my third the first time was when I delivered him via Caesarean section. I did my best to bond with him. We went to Ferrari World and rode all the rides, including the fastest roller coaster in the world. I ignored the warning that I couldn't ride, due to recent post-surgery. No more disappointments, mommy is strong. I noticed some changes though my baby had grown fast. He is now on his own.

Slowly, I'm getting my life back to normal. My colleagues are very supportive and do not rush me to do the same as we normally do. Kawkab was always there to protect me. She would not let me work. She did everything for me and just told me to sit at the computer, rest, or eat during break time. I hope all my colleagues feel the same, or else I'm guilty of receiving my salary without working hard for it. Back to work, I always get help. Ulfat is still there and she used to prepare my tea for breakfast. And, of course, my trio team who always got my back, I missed them, Joana purple back now in the Philippines and April now in Canada. They were always there, especially on my way to recovery. There were numerous photoshoots we used to have at work, outside, or at the park. And of course, the younger brother in the group, Darwin, turned out to be our cameraman. He was always ready to shoot our small gatherings, especially at work. He is the only one left now. My breaktime buddy.

I do have so many prayer warriors, especially from our nursing department, because I always see them in the church and even those belonging to other faiths, they always come to me and wish me healing. I wish I could mention them all here, but a page is not enough. The truth is, I only knew them by face, and only a few I know by name, but still, they prayed for me. I bet my colleague respected me, too, and they believed what I showed them was the real me; thus, I felt their love during those times; of course, we cannot please everyone, but clearly, my sickness brought peace to all of us. But as always, individual differences still divide us.

Through social media I aired my emotions, pains I felt and how I went through the effects of my treatment. I got to hear from those who were inspired which gave me the strength and courage to keep going. They might not know it but they inspired me too. I reconnected with friends and gained more friends. I conquered my sickness. And that is because God gave me a second chance. I need to discover my purpose.

I want to share what I wrote in my journal for my 50th birthday. My friend Joana and my colleagues organized a private party over the weekend at our workplace. My son and his friend were there too. All of those painful experiences never stopped from my diagnosis on August 14, 2011, until my third and last surgery, a day after my 46th birthday. I continue to fight and face the consequences that my sickness has brought me. Now, I can boldly say I am a survivor. A warrior, a fighter, a survivor for God.

19/12/2019

On December 20, 2016, five years after I was diagnosed with Stage 3 Breast Cancer, I was informed of the possible high risk of recurrence. I agreed to a Total Hysterectomy. Unfortunately, this medicine comes with bone and joint pains, obesity, poor eyesight, excessive sweating and more. But as I always say, life is a gift from God and it comes as a package. All we can do is accept it and live with it no matter what.

My life journey may not be the same compared to others. Most of us experienced difficulties and had been to the worst but for me I can say it's special. I will still continue to sail my boat through deep and shallow waters to live my life no matter how hard it may be. Until my final breath I will continue to inspire people and strengthen my faith to share myself and be a blessing to others.

What I've been through might be what I deserve, but where I'm going and leading in which direction should be what God deserves. I'm just looking forward to being with my son, living together, and catching up with the lost times. I just realized we lived apart alone for the past 13 years. It has been different for both of us since then.

BUT LIFE IS BEAUTIFUL, AFTER ALL! Thank you! (Dad & Mom) My beloved Family! Especially my son, who remained strong and had an unwavering spirit when I was at my weakest moment & to all the people who became part of my life's journey, good or bad! God Bless! Everyone

(DAISY LOZANO LUDAES, AUTOBIO)

Finally, I was back to normal work; I started to do shifts and, like everyone else, did everything without making excuses about my health condition. Everything was taken cared of carefully. God is good all the time. From the darkness, I found hope to hold onto. God sent me the rainbow to believe that there is more to life than sad memories and painful experiences.

I thank this country so much, the United Arab Emirates. There is no doubt that it's my home away from home, and it has saved my life many times. It is one of the best and safest countries to live in. "The Year of Tolerance" was promoted in 2019. It aims to foster respect, peaceful coexistence and mutual understanding among people in the UAE. I'm glad I have the chance to live here.

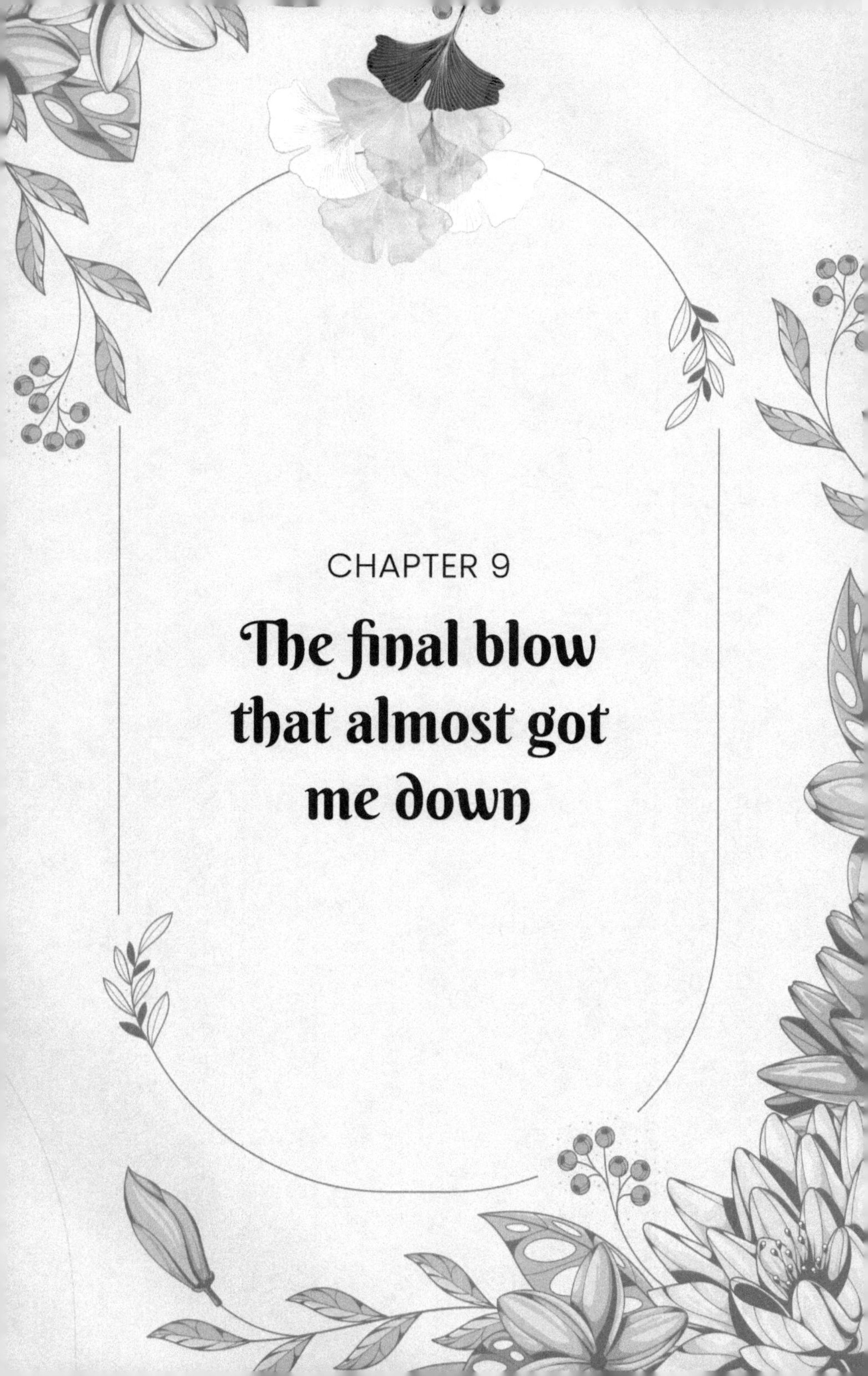

The final blow that almost got me down

It was at the middle of the pandemic when my son left for the US after working in the UAE for almost 3 years, I was left alone again. But I was so happy and excited with where my son's dream is bringing him. By then I feel accomplished already but not completely. Even though I tried my best to make up for the lost times, I can still feel the deep scars every time I see my son's eyes. All those were caused by my painful selfish decisions, especially not being there for him in his growing years. I know I can't do anything to change it. But I always pray and ask for forgiveness so that complete healing of the heart will come upon me and those I hurt, my loved ones.

Initially I thought of not adding this chapter in this book. I'm still in the process of rebuilding myself, picking up from the rubbles of destruction I recently created. But deep within me I have to do it, it may help others too. My book will not be complete without it. Everybody makes mistakes. All I need is to collect myself and present it as one whole new package. And I know that I'm ready to tell because my mind started to be cleared from worries. To borrow some words, it's like a cloud was sucked out of my mind and my brain started working.

But where to start and how to start. I was not ready at first to confront myself. It took me a few days to act. I know if I still go on it will be more difficult to get out of the situation. The financial gain I dreamt of will become a nightmare and not only that I will keep losing more money that are not even mine, and gain more debt. My only strength at that time was my Faith. But I know staying strong is not enough. God will provide but He can also say no or not yet time. He knows the desires of our hearts but He also does not like to put us in trouble let alone to suffer. I did not see it coming very soon, my decision to sell the shop, regardless if I lost more, but I'm glad I did. I was only able to convince myself to stop because I was already at the end of the rope.

My hope starts to dim, the light I was clinging to starts to fade away. After I lose everything, drown in debt, what will happen next? I have to do something and I know I cannot do it alone. Stress, worries and sleepless nights have taken its toll. It affected my voice and I thought I would lose it. I hardly joined my church choir. One day I woke up with back pain and then suddenly shooting pain towards my left leg until I could hardly walk. Pain reliever and therapeutic massage didn't work. For more than a month I ended up using a wheelchair at work from the entrance to the lab. All I can do is to pray and to ask prayers for healing. I avoided social media I stopped communicating and I alienated myself avoiding confrontations.

Earlier I was so happy with my son's success. He finally got what he had been praying for. I gave my blessing that now he can be totally independent as a grown-up man. It's now my time to look at my personal issues and start fixing my finances now that I have no one to support. I am so blessed with a family that instead of me helping them I am always the one being taken cared. So literally I'm on my own. I understand them, they only want me to take care of myself. After all I've been through, they are right. But I have always had that longing and it's not leaving me. I've played it many times in my mind. And what always comes out is my desire to be able to use my time and whatever resources I have to do something fruitful. Seems I'm looking beyond to find the purpose of my life. And in some ways to be able to pay forward given all the circumstances I've been through. I always thought I was always the receiving end of blessings. And my only wish is for me to have the means and perhaps I will be able to share with anyone in need.

For some time, I dismissed the idea. I still have a loan and credit card to pay. But my life has always been that way. It is not a show off but it is who I am. I help as much as I can. I will help as long as needed. I help because someone is in need more than me. And I help by not complaining or competing even though I know I deserve it because in my heart they need it more than I do whether they deserve it or not. And this is where my real trouble begins. I always end up doing more than expected sacrificing my time and space for everyone and I'm left alone to face my own. I can't keep going back, regretting and blaming myself or pointing out my mistakes. All I need to do now is fish out the learning part of each and every mistake. And start from there. How and what to avoid and take what is good.

It was in February 2022 I had a deal with private people who sideline as businessmen for a grocery shop. I did not plan properly and I did not do any consultation from anyone who knew about the business. Even my friends, much more than my family didn't know about it. That was my biggest mistake. I thought it was just a small thing and I can handle it so I need not involve or disturb them. I just had a clear goal in mind. I can only achieve if I will find a way to improve my finances, take risk and have an additional source of income or a business. One Filipina businesswoman just opened a restaurant on the ground floor of our building. I used to talk to her and she told me that she had other businesses earlier but unfortunately due to some circumstances especially during the Covid pandemic she was not able to sustain them. They survived by delivering foods passing as frontliners. I got inspired by her story of how she still keeps going on despite failures.

I sourced out funds and went on to buy the shop and even borrowed from friends and relatives. One big mistake I made was to borrow with big interest thinking I will be able to pay it immediately, I did not. I started paying for the bills and interest as soon as we made the agreement but they did not meet their due date of preparing the shop immediately for occupancy. I tried to understand that it was a normal delay but it took them long to make it ready. Worst the Trade License which was needed for us to open was not approved. Relying in good faith and wanting to avoid issues that might lead to misunderstanding. I thought it's ok, I can wait. I just need patience and things will be better. I did not see it as a red light.

It took me four months before I formally opened the shop. I lost a lot of money. I had Theresa and Harun alternating as cashiers. We still continued. Sales are not showing good, but I did try my best to save it. Four months after the opening, I was about to give up but then I found a business partner. He demanded 50% profit share but he only agreed to give 25% share from the full amount I bought the shop. He also did not comply with the 50% share in all dealings, purchases including expenses and purchases. Profit was not yet my concern at that time, we just started and actually we have to shell out from our pockets for needed expenses. I just realized that he was already expecting profit and he thought the money he initially added was enough and that's all he can give. I ended up taking care of all the expenses.

In between my work, I had to help in the shop. In my heart, with high hopes I can still work it out. Slowly I'm caught up with the interest I'm paying. The first six months I was able to manage with help from relatives and friends. But since I have to pay my obligations first, the budget for purchasing was sacrificed. I can't fill the grocery with as much as needed. Literally, it started to look empty. Customers always asked for discounts or cheap prices and since it was a close neighbourhood, they also came to take the goods only to pay it later. It got on and on and most of them unknowingly left the area and did not come back to pay. To add to that I was running the business as a customer and not as a business minded person. Not for profit but to make it affordable to the customer. I still have the list of collectibles now but I don't like the idea of going and knocking at their doors to collect them.

Before the end of 2023, suddenly I was caught up with everything, my attitude and attention at work was affected. And literally, I'm drowning in debt. Glad that not anyone has ever tormented me to pay. Guilt and shame affected me so much because I know they need their money back too. I tried to resolve it alone but with no money at hand it was so hard. I prayed for help and for one last time, God sent me names, one great friend overseas, whom I am guilty of because I failed her one time when she asked for help, she might not remember it. I was in Saudi when she called me. I was exactly in my room protesting for my delayed salary thus, I have nothing to send her but I did not tell her the reason. The other one is my relative, whom I did not even talk to for quite a long time. They sent me enough to get by and both prayed with me. I was able to managed whatever I could.

I'm not yet done. Last resort, I pawned my passport. This is the worst ever that I did. I remember years back then when in Hong Kong, using the passport as collateral was rampant. Someone asked to borrow my passport but I did not agree and she took it against me. When I loaned my passport, I thought of that situation. That's why she was angry at me that time because it really meant she did that because she was hopeless. I'm already on that stage, and if I do not do something to stop it, not only my self-respect but even my life I will lose it.

I was at work then, disturbed and I know I'm already losing it. Darwin, whom I always talk about work, life and my business over our break time, told me to put it "on sale" on social media, I did. Suddenly my message inbox was flooded. It was a big challenge for me, I need a good price to repay my debts. But it did not happen. Giving up something where I put my everything, sacrifices, sleepless nights and the shame that almost cost my life was very hard. I was caught in between. Nobody offered a good price. Everyone knows that I'm already hopeless so they are waiting only for me to give in to their offer. I have waited for two months since I posted. Paying the next bills and other expenses was the strong push to wake me up. There's no point holding on. It's no longer about pride and shame. It's all about my life, my purpose and what actually is God's will for me. Whether I will be paid enough or not I just have to let go. Give it to people who are ready to take over and hopefully to take care of it. But it's no longer my concern. I can't wait any longer, my anxiety is becoming more. Then from nowhere I got a buyer and I just agreed to their offer. The amount no longer matters to me. All I care about is to sell it and leave all the miseries behind.

But a few days later, one day before my birthday, I lost my phone, not an expensive one but to me the most precious gadget I only have. I lost all my contacts including the buyer I had to meet and supposed to close the deal with. My life was again turned upside down without my phone. I need it for work too, especially for my time in and out. But rather than panic I prayed for what the Lord wanted me to understand and just let go. I used my landline instead. I just let God work on it. I even forgot about my birthday but my friends did not. My birthday was celebrated with so much food as usual courtesy of my friends at home. It was truly happy after all despite the turmoil within me and after I almost lost everything. While my spirit is wandering, good things are also happening. I did blow my birthday cake. After all, life is like that.

Exactly Dec 23, 2023, they took over the shop although it was not yet fully paid. I was partly relieved and that same day, glad to see my brother Rommel and family come over to celebrate Christmas. It became a double celebration. I feel liberated. God gave me back my peace exactly on Christmas day.

It's not yet over. I still have to face the consequences. Worst scenario I can still expect. Obligations that are yet unsettled but the bulk of it, the heavy yolk I was carrying was fully lifted. Not only Christmas is Merry, I felt the real spirit and the meaning of the birth of Christ, I felt reborn. I'm liberated from my anguish and also because New year celebration is truly happy. It made me look forward to the rainbow after the storm. Not only me but especially my Family, my friends, my colleagues, I made them all happy. God gave me a new hope, a new beginning. Even losing my phone was meant to be. I can't help but worry still comes in between but I lift them all up to God. He will take care of things I cannot.

2 Cor: 9-10

But His answer was: "My grace is all you need, for my power is greatest when you are weak". I am most happy, then, to be proud of my weaknesses, in order to feel the protection of Christ's power over me. I am content with weaknesses, insults, hardships, persecutions, and difficulties for Christ's sake. For when I am weak, then I am strong.

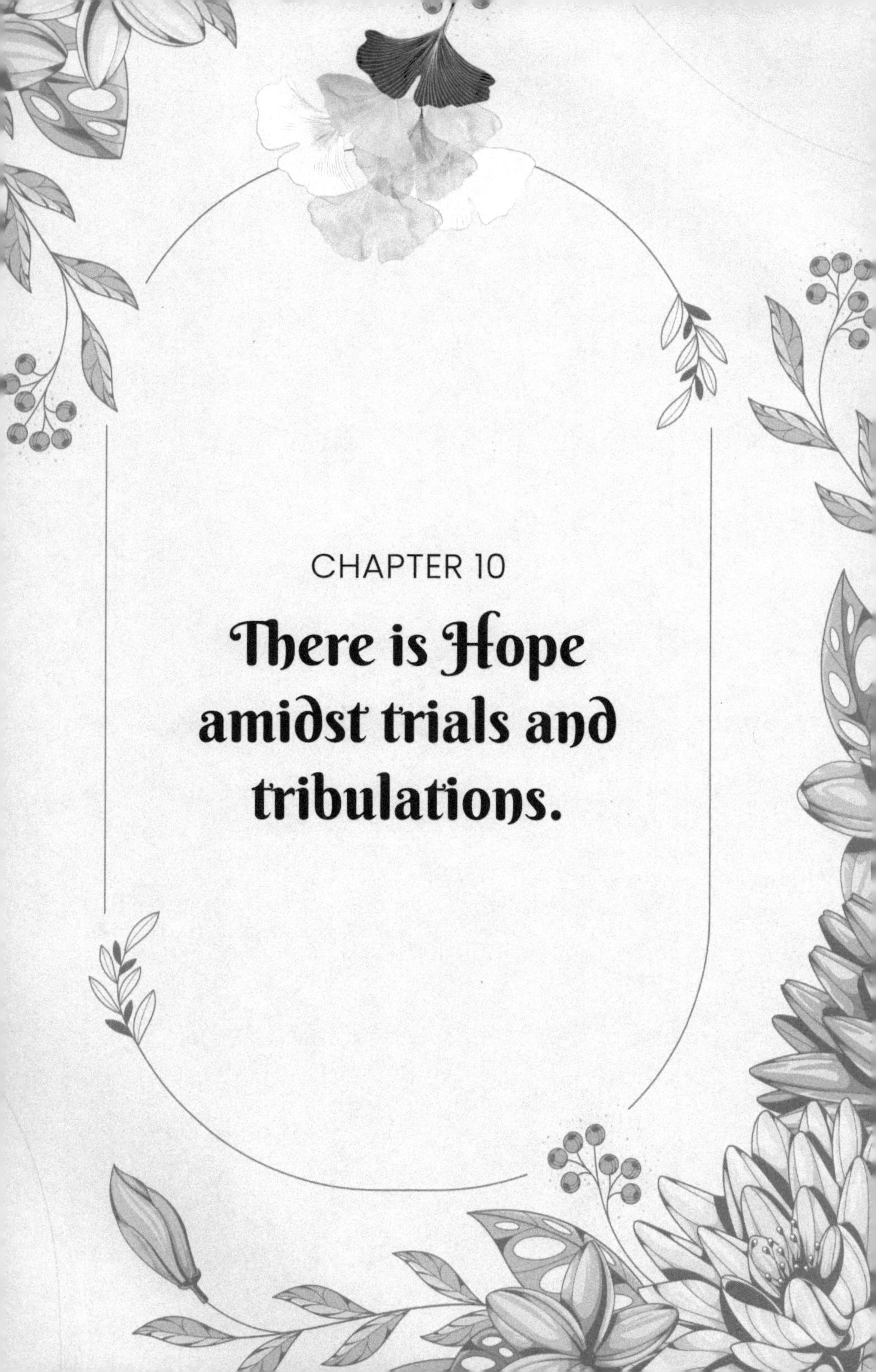

CHAPTER 10

There is Hope amidst trials and tribulations.

am a paramedic. I belong to the healthcare profession. Our mission is to take care of the health of the people but it's not a guarantee that I am spared of all those trials neither can I heal myself alone. But this time I experienced a feeling of relief! Great relief! It's unexplainable. It's still not over but I'm getting there. I trust God's way. I've pondered. I can't stop thinking how I allowed myself to suffer even though I'm already aware of the possible consequences because of the economic situation and was aggravated by the pandemic. I caused my misery but I still ask why this part of my life happened. I prayed for support, enlightenment and proper discernment but I still seemed confused. Only until I surrendered all my worries and fears as well as my joys and pains, much more my success and failures, that I felt a heavy weight was lifted up from inside. I start to notice again all my surroundings.

It was Sudden, everything came crashing in. My hope. My dream. It all disappeared in front of me. I can't remember anymore when I had a good talk, walked in the park or eat out with friends or colleagues. At first the feeling of letting go is too hard to bear but I had to go back to where I came from, remind myself of my goal, my purpose that there is still hope and only if I do that, I can be able to start all over again, a fresh start and this time leading to the right direction. This made me look back from my humble beginnings.

Back home, I take pride that I belong to the indigenous tribes of Northern Luzon. In the Province of Benguet, where I was born and raised. Where Baguio City, the Summer Capital of the Philippines is located. I'm the second of 6 children and the first of 3 girls. We were brought up in the usual family setting. My parents both came from poor and big families. Dad and mom were both working, they did everything to provide for us our needs and sent us to good schools and universities. Due to diligence and being hard working, they made sure we will not be lacking as they were before. They just need us to do our part and finish school in preparation for the best future.

While in high school, I can't remember what could have inspired me to consider entering the convent, except that I stayed in the dorm under the supervision of a nun and lived just next to the sisters' home. We did have our daily early morning and evening prayers as well as the daily morning masses aside from the usual regular Sunday masses. I'm not the typical good girl next door but I really thought I would be. Enrolment time for college started, that convent idea was put off. My mom asked me what to take up, I didn't have an answer and we were already within the campus to register so I just looked at the list of courses and I found what I just recently heard, B.S. Psychology without really knowing what is in that course. I learned to love it and I was ok with it but the following year I failed Inferential statistics. Honestly, I didn't understand anything at all. I tried to enrol in Nursing but I did not agree with the condition. I chose another University and enrolled in the Bachelor of Science in Medical Technology.

Since I'm just filling the gaps from my previous course, I used my free time to join the sports club. Since then, I've been competing locally. Not on the international level though because I'm still studying, I don't have time to train further to qualify. My mom would always stop me from going further for safety reasons. My sports career died a natural death. But I stayed connected with my team. I'm already working when I was inspired to study again. I took up Masters in Fiscal Administration. Motherhood came in between, I did not continue. Later on, I quit my job to take care of my son. When he was in grade school, I went back to study Bachelor of Laws. But I got distracted with my marital issues, I lost my interest and I just stopped going to school.

I almost lost myself after I got separated. I already admitted going abroad was my escape. It was a struggle. It took me years to get over it. Human as I am, I still made some wrong decisions in between. I asked for forgiveness and did amends. It was literally a twist and turn. But I got over it. We both made a mistake we admitted it and no more blame game. And we moved on. He married my friend's sister. My son took me for a date to inform me about it and we both were ok with it. He gladly embraced his younger step brother. I'm happy they get along well. I learned that being alone or having someone has an effect in a person's life but it is both a blessing in the right sense. Although even if it was a sudden event or it came as a surprise, there is no accident in entering into a relationship. It still needs to be given a thought, it has to be planned and both parties are prepared in their heart and mind. For whatever reason, don't rush. Same with being alone it is a gift. You can be happy too.

Grateful to God despite what I've been through, my work was not affected. It may be emotionally but I did not let it get in psychologically. My brain, though disturbed still worked and functioned well and I was able to deliver what is expected from me. I admit my performance slowed down but I still gave my best out from the struggles. It's been 17 years since I joined my work, I may not have achieved what I've been aiming for but I know I'm more blessed than what I deserve. My boss knows how much effort I'm giving and she appreciates it. I received work awards, several citation certificates and got a trophy too. I've supervised up to 42 staff and went beyond my scope of work giving lectures and orientations to other departments. Promotion has not yet come and may not happen. It might not be added in the list of my achievements but I'm good with it because more than the awards and rewards, from the way I work hard and help in many ways without expecting something in return I gained the respect from all my colleagues.

I told my boss that I'm writing a book and I asked her why one time she asked me, "why not write a book"? and went on to tell me how she liked the way and my style in writing communications and appreciated it more. I want her also to know that the freedom she gave me to be able to express myself and the responsibilities she assigned to me helped me to develop my skills and improve better.

A new chapter has opened in my life, I may falter again but I will not waiver, I will not change anything but I can still improve more to give the best in everything I do. I can't promise not to make mistakes and I may again face a wrong turn but I know better what to do. I can stand again each time I fall and be stronger. Because there is always the end of a dark tunnel where I can surely see the light. I can now boldly say, I'm back! I almost lost my self-confidence, self-esteem and the person who I am that I built over the years with God's grace. The shame almost got me. But God made me realize that there is no reason for Him to blame me, and let me down. I thought I can no longer be the same person, the daughter, sister, mom, auntie and the friend they look up to. I love my family but those times when I failed them, I avoided communicating because it caused me much pain and hurt me so much. My last recent vacation was for me the worst. No money, I'm unprepared and I carried the extra baggage of worries and stress. I can't fake it to show I'm good which made me look weird. I was not able to give time to my nephews and nieces, my son was not with us. I wish to be just like before with them. Spending more time together, enjoying each other's company, eating and going to places or watching movies. The only good thing I'm grateful for, I was with them physically even though my mind was out busy. I thought one day I will be able to redeem myself and I know with God's grace I will. I pray that they will remain grounded and will find their own success too in whatever path they may follow according to God's will.

I can say, in my own experience, Mental health is very important. When we are faced with great uncertainties and will hit rock bottom, we only needed strength and will power to survive. We have to take care of ourselves. We have to be physically, emotionally, and psychologically upright. Know when you can face your battle alone and when you need help.

Most people are ashamed to talk about it for fear of being misunderstood as having mental illness. But the more you keep it to yourself the deeper you go down. Don't conform to social standards and how they impose on what they like you to be. Stand your ground and be honest to yourself.

I saw this in social media reposted by a friend, "Fake it 'til you make it, necessary to keep a strong mind". I agree this will surely keep you going, but only for some time, the mind will soon get tired and needs rest too. Face your enemy whatever it is and confront it with reasons. Weigh the effects, is it beneficial? not only to you but to those involved. Does it cause division? then ask yourself, it's true you love what you do, but are you happy doing it, and are you sharing that happiness or your struggles? God wants only the best for us and not to let us suffer.

I know I'm not yet done. I will still continue to fight for good health. I still have some unfinished business, responsibilities to accomplish. Obligations to fulfil. I'm not even sure if I might have created enemies along the way while trying to climb up the ladder of success. And I can't postpone growing old. Days are passing as the clock is ticking. Above all no one knows the future, except the Almighty. We may have more time left in this world but the question remains if you only have one day left how would you want to spend it? It's your choice. Whether I have more days or one single day in my life I chose to restructure my life, my mindset and the way I look at things. I will continue to do what I do best and not according to my will but to the one who gave my life for free. In response, Live good. Live better. Live best. And share it to others. As the sole purpose of life is not to live for yourself but to live life for God, for yourself and for others.

Eph 6:13

"So put on God's armour now! Then when the evil day comes, you will be able to resist the enemy's attacks; and after fighting to the end, you will still hold your ground.

www.ingramcontent.com/pod-product-compliance
Lightning Source LLC
LaVergne TN
LVHW091056180726
843490LV00002B/521